NEIGHBEES

A LOOK AT LIVES IN THE HIVES

J. J. Lauria

authorHOUSE®

AuthorHouse™
1663 Liberty Drive
Bloomington, IN 47403
www.authorhouse.com
Phone: 1-800-839-8640

Published by AuthorHouse 2/2/2012

ISBN 978-1-4685-2520-5 (sc)
ISBN 978-1-4685-2519-9 (e)

Library of Congress Control Number: 2011962559

NEIGHBEES
INTRODUCTION--

Hi. Glad you stopped by. I've been meaning to tell you why those people across the street in that apartment complex seem so close to each other. This book could've been titled "Neighbors", but then that might not have caught your attention. "Neighbees" did. Who knew? But, you're in the Neighbee now! (Sounds sort of military, yes?)

Why "Neighbees"? Well, I think of Bees in a hive, and watching those busy bees, even if they're doing nothing--which is never--could become a national pastime or soap opera addiction. And yes, bother the bees and you can expect a reaction. But we won't bother them--just watch them in action making honey over there across the street, and listen to their key man, our narrator Stinko Ole, who at times thinks loud enough for us to hear him and other times talks as if he's talking to somebody, maybe a reader, never know; and then also you never know if we're liable to learn something from him and the other hive-occupants.

Jim

DEDICATION

Though not about them except in a peripheral and subliminal way, this book is dedicated to the NYPD, New York's Finest--from my limited and subjective perspective, the world's finest! Lifesavers, Peacekeepers, your best friends. Okay, so there are some bad examples, rotten apples in every bunch. That's life, and there are so few of those compared with the overwhelming number of good examples on the force. Surely among the ones we never see, are the roots that hold up the tree. But the ones we do, those who get our attention, are the ones in the trenches, who are challenged to live the NYPD motto, the ideal they aspire to: C P R-- Courtesy, Professionalism, Respect.

Not on the force? Then substitute "Love" for Professionalism, and aspire to C L R in all your service to Society, is that CLeaR? Almost? Good. Now, do what you can to be one of the finest: a real Neighbee!

Contents

CHAPTER ONE

We Do Courtesy, Love, Respect. Is that C L e a R? 1

CHAPTER TWO

My Neighbors' Peepers.. 5

CHAPTER THREE

Neighbee Tamara, I'll Find What I'm After 11

CHAPTER FOUR

Madame Backissue.. 19

CHAPTER FIVE

Where Tamara Yestadey Becomes To Me Yesterday But Not
X-ed Out Completely On My Calendar 25

CHAPTER SIX

The Doombrowski's 29

CHAPTER SEVEN

Oh, And Also Beware Of Dirty-Minded Boobies................................ 35

CHAPTER EIGHT

Holy Smoke With Scrabble And Sydelle 41

CHAPTER NINE

Chief Orville Late-Lee Earlie Speak Wisdom 47

CHAPTER TEN

Of Rats And Women And Flaming Fiddlers 55

CHAPTER ELEVEN

The Bulgarian Bulge 63

CHAPTER TWELVE

The Iceman Cometh & Goeth 69

CHAPTER THIRTEEN

Umberto Loves Alba Madonna In The Bathtub 77

CHAPTER FOURTEEN

Holy Hotski.. 83

CHAPTER FIFTEEN

Who's The Man? 89

CHAPTER SIXTEEN

No Tello Rutuolo & Also That Vassily-o Fellow 95

CHAPTER SEVENTEEN

El Pranko & Rutuolo The Fig-Dealer... 101

CHAPTER EIGHTEEN

El Hammo & The Backfiring Boffo 107

CHAPTER NINETEEN

In The Pincus.. 113

CHAPTER TWENTY

Room For Neighbees, Mushrooms, And Foster Children................ 119

These are neighbees, some are fat, some are skinny,
some short, some tall, and some are even dogs.
after having moved, they become Gone.

CHAPTER ONE

We Do Courtesy, Love, Respect.
Is that C L e a R?

Hello folks, I'm Stinko Ole, as you just read. Now, all the words in this book are mine except for things I report others have said. Even though they're my words, they've been scrubbed--I guess that's the way to say it--of my Brooklynese spelling and speaking, pretty completely. In other words, instead of "shootin' the breeze" or "Ya know?", it will be shooting and you. But this doesn't mean anybody's going to shoot you, if you get my drift. Now, that's another thing we're working on: to say something else instead of "drift". Maybe "metaphorical impression", but don't get your hopes up. Maybe I'll go for "M.I."--I don't know, we'll see. Just grasp that I'm smarter than I sound, even if I do say so myself.

Now, sooner or later, all of us are going down the drain, you know, the sewer? Physically, that is, but when we stick together, it's harder for that to happen. We become like leaves that don't get washed down with the rainwater and all the other juices that flow in the gutter, get me? Instead of "Goodbye forever old fellows and gals...", we clump together, stuck on the drainholes of the steel sewer grate at the end of the curb gutter in the street--that's the point of "Neighbees". If you want to live in the building, sorry, you have to wait for a vacancy. But hey, don't make a scene, just do the Neighbees thing in your own home and Nabe, and watch how eventually you'll be liable to almost stop up the sewer having formed a clump yourself!

1

Now, I don't think that bird who wrote the Introduction can hear me, but what the hey? So what? Let's get down to Neighbees: Of all the women in my dissipated life, there stand out three and they are each someone else's wife--no complaints from me. I'm talking about Drinkie Saluna, Isabella Slutta, and Tamara Yestadey (this weird name is not pronounced like "Yes, Daddy." but like the day before today).

We were fast friends, like clumps of wet and dry leaves stuck together on the drainholes of the steel sewer grate at the end of the curb gutter in the street. My stoop was our frequent haunt. Drinkie and me could spend hours warming those concrete steps, just shooting the breeze, stopping it in mid-air, like we just hit a flying brown bear. "Hello Stinko!" she'd say, to begin our session of the day, for that was my name: Ole! Like those walking sombreros shout down Mexico way when de bool almost hooks the onions off that foppish-looking Toreador in the embroidered yellow and gold pantyhose-ay with the red cape, and what could I say? I had to keep the conversation in play, so "Muy Buenos Dias, Amiga mio!" got us underway, setting us off like clumps of wet and dry leaves stuck together on the drainholes of the steel sewer grate at the end of the curb gutter in the street.

Once in a while, I'd look her way and say, "Drinkie Saluna," summoning forth all the pent-up emotion of affection and admiration for her attempt at sociability, "If Isabella Slutta and Tamara Yestadey were here with us today, you know, you and me? Then, they'd feel what we feel about everything going on here and everywhere else. You know what I mean? Do you get what I say, Drinkie Saluna--do you really get my drift? I'm talking to you like a tree giving away its Autumn leaves. Are we connecting here? And she'd look at me through that sky-blue right eye with the raised eyebrow, not the greenish-brown left one with which she'd frequently wink at policemen, firemen, and Carmelo, the postman with the shorts and nice knees--her words not mine. And what do you think she'd say? Well, nothing right away. But then, that smile, replying "Stinko, you're the man. There's only one real Stinko, and that's you. You're the man, and I'm the woman, and they be our Neighbees all around us, and I get your drift the same way my husband, Fulmuna gets your drift when he sits here with you most nights, the two of you fast friends like clumps of wet and dry leaves stuck together on the drainholes of the sewer grate at the end of the curb gutter in the street!"

Wow, that was real heavy! Not the words, which could probably make you think there was nothing going on in either of our heads--tell me you're not thinking that right now! Nothing to say? Okay for you. What was heavy was the passion behind the old cliches. Yes, clean "neighbee-passion"! Try it sometime instead of laughing at us. Okay, so you're not laughing.

Anyway, these were some of the neighbees with whom I found favor, and they with me, covering some of the smooth concrete of the seat-warmed stoop all my dissipated life.

What more could one want, but to surround himself with such neighbees? Yes, fast friends, like clumps of wet and dry leaves stuck together on the drainholes of the steel sewer grate at the end of the curb gutter in the street.

It just don't get any better--not better, no way Hose-ay!

This neighbees thing is Love, Courtesy, and Respect, not like the NYPD who does Professionalism instead of Love--they have to. Of course, they do Courtesy first, then Professionalism, then Respect: "CPR" Get it? They do CPR, unless you're really dead in which case they spell it out and maybe draw a chalkline around the dead body, and now they give you a choice of pastels instead of just white; but don't take that to the bank. Maybe that chalk stuff is just for TV. The NYPD is not into Amateurism, but Professionalism--it's not CAR, but CPR, and they drive it home with class! Try getting arrested sometime and watch them in action--they're pro's at it, even give you a pair of cufflinks to try on. Who else does that for you?

Some neighbees are Peeping Toms,
men Peepers and women Peepers,
but MOSTLY men, for some strange
reason, having To do with how Their
eyes work.

CHAPTER TWO

My Neighbors' Peepers

Hi again, it's me, Stinko Ole, who else? You know, Ole, like those walking sombreros shout down Mexico way when de bool.......... Remember? The horns almost harvesting the onions off.......um. Anyway, I don't like to repeat myself, as if by now you don't know that, if you get my drift. I'm talking to you like a tree giving away its Autumn leaves. Are we connecting or what?

Anyway, I told you about Drinkie, remember? Yes, Fulmuna's wife-o. By the way, "Drinkie" is a nickname. Her official name is "Dorinka", and don't ask me why Italian parents name their daughter that, unless one of them had a Russian Grandmother for who she was named. Now do you follow my Jeopardy clue?

Okay, well, this is still about the Saluna family--"couple"--that I should say because all the kids are big on their own now, you know what I'm saying? By the way, that name Saluna got to you, yes? I know it. I understand from Drinkie's other Grandpa that when they got off the Mayflower and landed on Ellis Island--who knows what the boat was named? I'm sure the city has a record, but anyway, the name was Calunia, and the drunken immigration guy, who probably couldn't spell either or understand Italian, somehow put down Saluna, you know, like probably where the dumbo had lunch, and bingo! Done! Finito!, like Umberto says. Don't worry, I'll tell you about him too, he also lives here. I'm talking about Umberto, who's "Finito"?

Well, watch this twist like we did last summer--that's just a little nostalgic humor I threw in to make a pleasant talk, you get my drift? Okay, here we go: I say goodnight to Drinkie, a little hug and a cheek to cheek sort of kiss so the neighbees who see can write their own soap if they're inflaming themselves with all that porno crap they dull their senses with--you get the picture? I have one particular guy in mind here and we'll be talking about him, you'll see.

So, I'm waiting for Fulmuna to appear. One whole hour! There I am, alone on those concrete porch steps. It was muggy and I sat so long I was afraid if I got up suddenly, I'd be leaving some cloth from my raggy fatigues stuck to the concrete, you know, everything sticks to you when it's sweaty like that. I think it's the enamel concrete paint that does it. I should have sat on the New York Post instead, or even the Daily News, you know what I'm talking about? Suddenly, like a nervous, nauseous squirrel, who's afraid to jump from the tree whose branches scrape a sixth floor bedroom window in the court, I hear this buzzing and clicking, buzzing and clicking. So I look up and what do you think I see? Take a guess, you'll never get it--but guess anyway: Nothing! Then a walk through the short lobby to the court--more buzzing and clicking. It's the squirrel up in the tree of the court! And what's bugging him: buzzing and clicking coming from the court roof! Fulmuna! leaning over the edge, sounding like the squirrel! What is he up to? Teasing the tree-rat? What gives? Fulmuna, big as life, much, much bigger also than a scaredy-pants squirrel looking for nuts in all the wrong places!

Anyway, I get a little annoyed 'cause he's supposed to be down here on the stoop with me--not that he has to, but that's what neighbees do, you know what I mean? We're fast friends like clumps of wet and dry leaves stuck together, etcetera, etcetera, etcetera, these last three words like Yul Brynner in "The King And I"--I just say that, you get it? Probably don't even know who is Yul Brynner. Why should you unless you're old or like old stage or movie musicals. This is nostalgic humor, make it interesting--that's the way to talk! Hope you know what "nostalgic" means--not everybody does.

But then, I see he's got the spyglasses with him, and usually Isabella is down here with us for a while anyway 'til Boobie, her husband, comes home for midnight lunch before going back to the train yards on the early a.m. shift. But tonight, she's not--I don't know if they call it "The Graveyard", but it's not too far from the old Gravesend cemetery a few blocks from here, you know?

Sometimes, Boobie leaves out the "f" in that word "shift", because he hates the hours, and she don't like that dirty talk, even though "Slutta" is her last name. But her maiden name was "Hooker", and now, doesn't that show you why you can't go by somebody's name all the time or none of the time, you get the picture?

Well, Isabella is a looker, you know what I mean? And I'm thinking this looker whose name was Hooker and now is Slutta, but far from the gutter, in that sixth floor apartment, is taking a shower at the midnight hour, and Fulmuna is enjoying the water games, get it? So, with that Columbo thought--used to be Sherlock Holmes, right?, I hightail it up to the roof, and there, with the spyglasses hanging off his wrist is Fulmuna with empty arms--that's a little Frank Sinatra joke--great song--he really did it good a long time ago: Full moon, and empty arms, la da da da, da la da da dee da dee dum...... . So, a little out of breath, me that is, Fulmuna, I find out, is not a peeping tom but instead, a "sleeping tom"! Then, I get afraid he's going to let go of those spyglasses, and also I'm starting to think he's just a stargazer like an astronomer, whatever. But I look and see. It's his own bathroom window! and who's in there showering in all her delicious glory? It's his wife, Drinkie--wow! So that's it! He's peeping on his old lady and she's a sight too! But, we're neighbees, you know, like clumps of wet and dry leaves--don't let me say it again. And me and Drinkie? Sure, it's love, but it's love and respect and courtesy, you know? Like the NYPD only instead of love they do Professionalism. Good stuff, right? So, there we are: I love Drinkie very much, and with her Fulmuna out, like right next to me, I want to take a peek, or say, "peep", so, I try to gently raise the binoculars to look at Drinkie and stoop down 'cause the strap is wound around his thick wrist. There, with one eye closed, ooh! what a sight! She's showering but wearing a bathing suit! I don't care--she's showing me nothing you can't see at the beach, if you get my drift. "Beach drift"! Right? Now I don't feel so guilty, but I wonder about Fulmuna. He knows what she looks like without the suit. Anyhow, it was too much for my brain.

Suddenly, Fulmuna sneezes, and courteous fool that I am, like a reflex, I say, "God Bless you!" He wakes up: "Stinko! What the hell is going on? How did you get me up here, and with those binoculars?" "Fulmuna, Fulmuna," I say, "We're supposed to be stoop-ed people, not 'roof-roosters' with spyglasses! Is that what keeps you up all night?"

"Wait! Get down!" he says, "There she is!" Crouching down I see Isabella Slutta on the sixth floor looking up from the darkened kitchen window with her binoculars. Fulmuna says, "She's got the hots for me, I'm sure of it. She knows I'm here but is making like she's interested in Pluto

7

and Uranus or 'Ura-nus'--ah, either way I say it I get in trouble." So, I ask him: "Fulmuna, do you catch Isabella in the shower from here? Looks like a good view." "Oh yeah," he says, "but she also wears a bathing suit." "Wow! How then," I ask, "do they get clean with that on? I don't know about this, Fulmuna, why don't you give her a break and let her know when you're not watching. That is, if she can trust you. I mean, you say 'Goodnight' on the stoop, and what do you do? Come up here to glimpse the girl in the wee hours! Oh man!" "Stinko, I don't need to do that, because Isabella also takes baths and it's a pretty good view from here with no bathing suit!" he whispers, like with his peeping eyes glowing under the light of the full moon. Hah! Fulmuna under the full moon! Only once in a century do those two astral bodies come that close in a sentence! "So, there you go Ful. Bingo!" I tell him. "No 'bingo' Stinko, because it's a bubble-bath. I only see her like a strobe light shot, if you get the picture!" I plead, "These be our neighbees! What would Boobie say if he found out?" Then, Fulmuna lays it on me real weird. "Stink, he knows. He's the one who told me I could look if I let him look at Drinkie--he likes her bod with a capital 'B'. Fair enough? By the way, these are her spyglasses." I said, "Fulmuna, are you nuts? What's next, 'Wife-swapping'?" "No way!" he tells me, "We're 'neighbees', to use your made-up language. You know, like clumps of wet and dry leaves stuck together on the drainholes of the steel sewer-grate at the end of the curb gutter in the street. No, Stinko, the line is drawn, as you also say, with my old lady. It's love, respect, and courtesy. So, I told her, Boobie is a voyeur, you know what that is, right Stink?" "Of course I do," I tell him, "it's someone with roving eyes like on a sight-seeing voyage, and he looks in all the cabin windows at night." So he says "Now doesn't that sound more classy than 'Peeping tom'? I tell her that way because it sounds less sneaky or snoopy, Stink. So I told her it's okay to give Boobie a glimpse, just sponge-bathe before you shower, then put on your Bikini before getting in the shower--you'll be modeling--it'll be like dessert for Boobie after he has his midnight lunch. Isabella doesn't have a clue that he's watching Drinkie, and to show Boobie how neighborly I am, he's got my Bausch & Lomb fieldglasses, which he says beat his, so we switched--it was worth it to me, his do just fine from here. He's gonna be looking for mine as soon as he has his midnight lunch, it's getting to be a reflex, and also--" "Hold on, Ful! Let me get this straight," I interrupted, "Drinkie knows she's being watched by the Boob, but Isabella thinks only Boobie is watching Isabella?" His eyes lit up like they were part of the night sky: "Yeah, that's how it works!" he said, chuckling, or more like "cackling",

I should say, with a big Fulmuna smile with the spaces between his top choppers.

"Fulmuna," I tell him, "you guys are a special sick kind. I don't know how you survive all winter, especially up here!" And what answer does he give me?

"Stinko, it's like the beach, you gotta wait for warm weather to get eye-exercise, but we don't mind suffering for a worthy cause. And that don't stop us from being good neighbees, like clumps of wet and dry leaves stuck together on the steel sewer grate--". And then I spoke in unison with him as if we were a duet at the naval academy in Moscow singing Russian sailor songs: "at the end of the curb gutter in the street."

Well, anyway, I knew instead of being "stoop-ed", we'd be roofed that night, which wasn't so bad except I like the concrete steps better when I warm them with my back parts--how do you like that clean language?--but not on sticky nights. Maybe there's hope for me to step up in class after all, no ass or butt talk for me, no way! I'm more sophisticated than when I was young and unsophisticated. I was stupid then and it wasn't spelled "stoop-ed"! Don't give me that "inexperience of youth" stuff--notice I didn't say "crap"? All young people are stupid until they get smart. I know it hurts, but too bad. Say it now: stupid! Again: stupid! One more time: stupid! There! Now you've got the picture, and believe me, if you became one of my neighbees, you'd get love, courtesy, and respect, not like the NYPD who does Professionalism instead of love--they have to, that's what they're all about, and pretty darn good at it--notice I didn't say "damned"? Same thing, of course, but less coarse, because as you know, I'm more sophisticated, and hate repeating myself, too.

So, that's what good neighbees do--got it? Now, you remember the Russian navy singing? Doesn't that "navy" sound like neighbee? Don't say maybe. You hear that similar sound? So, I'm not that weird when it comes to making unauthorized analogies! Maybe just a little out to sea. More in chapter three.

Yes, that's what good neighbees do--though I hate to repeat myself. It just don't get any better--not better, no way Hose-ay! Now, for Chapter 3.

Neighbee Tamara, I'll Find What I'm After

Oh, you're still here? Waiting, I guess, for Chapter 3, right? I knew it--just testing. Get my drift? Now, you gotta know how things are with me and Tamara. First of all, did you catch the chapter title? If you were singing that old love ballad by Anthony Newley, "Who Can I Turn To?", you'd be able to fit it into one of the lyric phrases: "Maybe tomorrow, I'll find what I'm after...", and that fits also with what I'm laying out in this chapter about Tamara Yestadey today. Why now? Because, because, because tomorrow is too long to wait, and yesterday is too late.

Listen, the two of us are neighbees, but more than that, we're part of the eligible unlonely-but-open-to-consider-holy-matrimony-crowd. Do you get what I'm trying to say? To call us "Singles" is an insult as if you're brushing off a piece of American cheese that fell on the floor before being slapped on some sprouted whole wheat bread slice, lightly toasted, because you don't want to ingest--fancy word for swallow, but don't let it distract you--whatever mites it picked up down there or any plastic particles from the wrapping machine at the processor plant. They're only machines, you know, and they make mistakes like the humans who designed and built them, and are run by people that make mistakes, but because they're machines we don't say "mistakes" for that sounds like humans, and we don't want people to be reminded that the humans who made the machines are responsible, so, when the machine goes on the fritz, it's a "malfunction", get it?

People make mistakes, but machines fritz up, so you can't blame a person for a machine mistake, because the machines don't make mistakes, they malfunction, so fritz gets the blame, get my drift? I hope so because otherwise, I can't go on. It would be a mistake to continue, unless I were a machine, in which case it would be a malfunction.

Now, where were we? Oh yes, Tamara. Tamara, Tamara, what can I say about Tamara Yestadey today that I didn't say yesterday--that's "yester", got it? Good! Well, here's how it sets up:

Me and Tamara like each other. We're neighbees, you know, like clumps of wet and dry leaves stuck together on the drainholes of the sewer grate at the end of the curb gutter in the street. That's kind of poetic, yes? By now, you should have picked that up, just like we do not often enough, from that sewer grate so the rainwater doesn't stop up down the whole block like a beaver dam in the concrete jungle right in front of these apartment buildings. Do you get the picture? Good.

So, you know me, never attached--let's not do the American cheese thing, so forget the "S" word that is followed by "in" which spells "sin", and you're only halfway through the word "single"but it's a pretty good clue if you know where I'm going with this, which is there are some people who confuse the two.

Now, I'm no saint, which by the way also has "sin" in it if you take away the "a" and "t", and saint is where I ain't at, but I'm not big on sin, so let's just take the "i" and let that be me, got it? I hope you get the picture, cause as you know I hate to repeat myself, got it? Good.

I'm an "okay Joe". Had a few close calls with some hot stuffed sandwiches, if you catch the food picture. Yeah, delicious stuff, but always left me wanting to wash my hands, greasy, real greasy girls. And all I mean is they were sticky as far as emotions go. I couldn't see myself smart enough to deal with all those emotional fragments hanging off the hero, you know, peppers and eggs, some onions that missed the chop before Stromboli's chef threw them in the pan with the exploding oil beads or water beads or whatever the little pings are that burn the back of your cooking hand and stain the corduroy slacks that whistle when you walk. I really think those guys should cook wearing safety glasses, the way they heat up all that extra virgin olive oil--it's a waste, too, if that pops out of the pan--then nobody gets it, got it? Good. Let's not talk about Las Cucarachas, okay? But Stromboli's has never been closed up, so maybe they take care of that, or take care of somebody, if you get my drift, yes? Good. So, I never got too deeply involved with these chicks, and believe me, something hot was on the stove with us, because after a few of them were married for years, I got a call--same phone number. I never moved, and one was divorced, another separated, and another I don't know what. All but one had kids or a kid and they just wanted to know what I was doing. I think I know what that means. Do you get my drift? Don't make me repeat myself, which I hate to do. Got it? Good.

I've gotta thank Drinkie for keeping me out of trouble. She said they're not for me, unless I just want to wear out my plumbing--yeah, that's the way she talks--she makes pictures with her words. I know, you're thinking she's saving me for herself even though she's got Fulmuna. But it's more than that. We have for each other, love, respect and courtesy, almost like the NYPD, right? I told you already about them. That's what neighbees do, like clumps of wet and dry leaves stuck together on the drainholes--okay, enough, you know the rest.

So, here we are, with me, or should I say "I" like the middle letter in saint--and yes, at last, Tamara Yestadey, all neighbees, all living on the fifth and sixth floor except I'm on the first, which is why I'm stooped, spelled s t o o p e d with no "u", or even clearer, with no "me" in it! I could hop out my front window to those concrete porch steps except for the steel fence pickets, which make me think of the foppish-looking toreador in the embroidered yellow and gold panty-hose-ay with the red cape, and suddenly I'm thinking spiked onions like on the horns of not a dilemma, but the bull, and that's not the cops, but a toro, as the walking sombreros say down Mexico way, and now I'm thinking I'd better count the crops, not mine but the ones in the fridge because I'm gonna need them when I make sauce tonight. Yes, Stinko Ole makes the best tomato sauce probably on the East Coast, and to prove that, just ask Tamara, who says my culinary skill--that means cooking talent--is a gift from God. Of course, why not? She gets a quart of sauce from me once a month when I make a pot the size of my toilet bowl. But don't think she and I connect only because of that. You might as well think she'd like to change "Yestadey" to "Ole" so she wouldn't have to wait for the elevator to her upper floors apartment. Listen, she's not a divorcee yet. Her old man left her because he was sort of kinky, if you get the picture. He collected dirty magazines, and the more she threw out, the more he brought in.

Then I think he tried to get her involved with wife-swapping--real pig, if you follow my swine song, so that was it. They split a few years ago, no kids, but she still uses that name "Yestadey"--how sad, like the song "Yesterday". Better than her maiden name, though. Guess what that is! No, forget it--you'll never guess: it's "Sleighme!" Can you imagine? Tamara Sleighme! And get this: it's pronounced "slimey". Spelled like in a one-horse open sleigh, with a "me" for a tail! Don't ask. Maybe it's Finnish like where the Reindeers grow. You know, Reindeers like in Santa Claus? Who knows? I don't ask questions. But, "slimey" sounds like hell, and I guess she could pronounce it "sleighme", but that would sound like an invitation to commit murder.

Anyway that should have been his maiden name instead, but I guess he'd be reading different magazines if he were allowed a maiden name, if you get my drift. All I know is she likes me and always seems to stiffen up when she sees me with Drinkie on the stoop. I think she and "Hottie" are still married and he's not coming back, but who knows? Listen, you know how I know there's something cooking with us? One day, she comes to the door when I'm making sauce--she smelled it, and that means a quart-sized mason jar for her. So, she asks me how old I am and I told her forty-six, which was eight years ago. She then told me she was fifty-two, or six years older than me. That makes her sixty now to my fifty-four. Doesn't look it though, right? No wrinkles, yeah, prematurely gray hair, no makeup, a little bottom-heavy, but not really out of shape, and calloused knees from all that praying she does, I guess. I'm a knee-noticer.

So there we were, neighbees, like clumps of wet and dry leaves stuck together on the drainholes of the steel sewer grate at the end of the curb gutter in the street. And she stands by the bedroom door and says, "Stinko, that's a king-size bed!" So, I'm starting to feel a little sweaty, if you know what I'm saying, and I'm thinking about one of those greasy pepper and eggs heros with all the sticky emotional fragments, if you get the picture. So, I said, "Now you know how big mine is, how big is yours?" And with that she snapped like a rubber band stretched out to bind three dozen Hustler magazines like her husband, Hotalova, used to collect. Funny name, hah? And it was pronounced "Hot all over" just like you would read it phonetically. And boy, did she ever blow her cork, if you know what I'm saying, like a champagne bottle on New Year's Eve when all the drunken celebrants in Times Square watch the ball drop, and pluck their index fingers from their mouths to make that popping sound. Here, stop reading for a moment and try it yourself--it will be hard to stop, but eventually you have to so you can find out what happened to Tamara before today becomes yesterday and you have to wait until tomorrow. Okay, that's enough.

So, she says to me--I never forgot the words, because at that moment when she came in, I forgot to turn off my old Sony cassette tape recorder which I put on to catch a Sinatra song I was playing from an old 45 rpm record so I could take it with me to play on the stoop. The song was "You'll Never Walk Alone", you know, from "Carousel", the Rodgers and Hammerstein musical? So, here's what's on there: Tamara says, "Stinko, that's a king-size bed!", and I say my stupid thing which was really curiosity about her bed because I remember when the porno-master, Hotalova, took off, he asked me if I wanted to buy some king-sized fitted bedsheets, never used, and he said he had thirty sets which he'd sell me for a hundred bucks. That's about three bucks and change each set! But, I didn't bite because I thought he'd return and also didn't know if she knew what he was doing, and besides, I only change my sheets when the seasons change. So, my saying "How big is yours?" was an innocent question. I swear on my dead grandmother's grave at Greenwood cemetery overlooking the Narrows Bay, best view in Brooklyn, and they have nice tours there but don't ask me where her stone is. Oh, I didn't tell you the unforgettable words she says. Guess. What do you think she hits me with, verbally that is? Take another guess. Oh, you didn't take the first one. Anyway, uh,no, forget about it, you can't imagine. I have it on the tape. I don't know why I keep it but who knows? Maybe the psychiatrist, if I ever have need for one, but I don't think so because my gut feeling is they all need help, especially with making up names for all these behaviors people have been doing for centuries around here. What did she say? I can't forget: "Stinko, I thought I could trust you, but now I see you're no different from all the rest: Hotalova, Fulmuna, and Boobie. All you men have is one thing on your mind and you're all going to Hell. You think a jar of tomato sauce is the price of admission to my private parts? There's much more to me than animal passion. You don't have a clue what real love is all about!" And I think I remember every word. With that she left my apartment and bad enough the echo of those firedoors can wake you out of a dead sleep, this one shook even my concrete floor! Yes, she slammed it! Well, we made up after that because I had Drinkie Saluna bring her the sauce and a note explaining that I was just curious to know the size of her bed because if she threw it out when she redid the apartment, and replaced the mattress King Porno Hotalova soiled, it might be a queen-sized one. So, guess what? Drinkie saved the day. She tells Tamara that as neighbees our motto is Love, Respect, and

Courtesy, like the NYPD, except they do Professionalism instead of love. And then she pops the question, not like the champagne bottle cork on New Year's eve that I just gave you a chance to imitate--try it again if you want--but the size comparison, and what do you know? Tamara starts in on Drinkie as if she's coming on to her like a Lesbian! So, Drinkie, good soul that she is, tells Tamara that even Lesbians can be good neighbees if they practice the motto of Love, Respect, and Courtesy, like the NYPD except they do Professionalism instead of love, which really might be love in another sense of the word--let's hope so.

I think a lot of those Lesbees do the neighbee thing, but they get lumped together with the Dikeamagoolas and so get their lumps by association.

And so, from Tamara's lips comes the answer I hoped for: Queen-sized! That was it. Look at all the scungille about nothing that comes from a little misunderstanding! Good thing she wasn't the Queen of England back in the days when you could get two fresh heads from the Tower of London for a shilling, and maybe wrapped--they're less messy to carry that way.

Drinkie then tells Tamara that if she still has the thirty sets of king-sized, I'll pay two hundred bucks for them. And that was it! Then Drinkie tells me all was forgiven and Drinkie is willing to kick in a hundred of her own for fifteen sets of the sheets! And what do you think she told me? "Stinko, you told me you only change your sheets four times a year, so, at that rate you'll be dead by the time your four sets are ready for the rag heap. I can use half of these, which means you paid six bucks instead of three for fifteen sets you're never going to use!" How could I argue with a practical woman? Besides, Drinkie told me she changes hers so often that she'll buy my fifteen for ten bucks each, which would give me a profit of fifty bucks! Guess what happened. No, don't guess, you won't get it. All this math makes me sleepy, so I gave Drinkie a "C" note and said keep all the sheets for yourself. It was worth one hundred buckaroos to restore my trust with Tamara. I learned these fancy money-words from television gangster movies.

As they say, "All's well that ends well." And then, Tamara invites me to a dinner at her pad. So, what do you think she serves? Shrimp ravioli with my tomato sauce, which has meat in it! That's a "no-no" for me, but for the sake of being neighbees, you know, Love, Respect, and Courtesy, like the NYPD except they do Professionalism instead of Love, I eat the things, hoping she will mistake my grimace for a smile. Now, that's the one reason I think people who do dinner parties should have a dog. He eats, I fast from Shrimp ravioli, and Tamara knows nothing, so everybody's happy, but because she's allergic to dog hair, there's no dog, and I play the part and everybody's still happy, though with me, not so much.

CHAPTER FOUR

Madame Backissue

I think leading up to the straw, you know, the last one, all that camel's back stuff? I'm talking about Tamara and her hotski husband, Hotalova before the split--had to happen. It certainly threw a big log on the fire--hope you're catching all the code language. It makes facts fancy things, I think.

It happened three days in a row. There I was, dozing on the stoop and Drinkie gives me the elbow in the ribs--and oh, she has pointy elbows: "Stinko! Stinko!" she says in a stage whisper, you know, the kind that the person you don't want to hear something hears because you're whispering loud enough? "What? What?" I asked, shocked out of my serenity. "Look! Look who's coming! It's Madame Backissue!" she says, then tries to act like she's oblivious to the one-woman sanitation truck coming toward our buildings. Two big plastic bags are balanced on her 4-wheel shopping cart crammed with bundles of magazines and paperbacks.

Must have been a nice-looking woman once. Even now, not bad--I guessed her good for sixty, maybe more; but a little makeup, a clothing change--or burning, a bit of hair color, and you've got a nice-looking hoarder! Three rooms on the second floor were too little for her--she was maxed out. I knew because Grandpa Bert went in there to fix a toilet tank leak a few years ago, and told me he had to fight his way through two rooms and an inner hall of printed matter almost reaching the ceiling! He told her next time she'd have to hire someone to move bundles of magazines out of the tub because they were in the way of his elbow and shoulder and it wasn't his job to move stuff to do a plumbing repair--and he was old even then, if you get my drift about oldness--it's in my mind, never in his!

Her real name is Gretchen Collins. Tamara used to call her Gretchen Collyer. You know why? I thought not--how could you? These things were before your time and mine too. But maybe you're older and read about them: the Collyer brothers. They like died in the late 1940's--two brothers who lived in a brownstone, up in Harlem, and back then, they were about the only white guys living there! They were found dead in the place. One, when he was tunneling through tons of garbage to bring food to his paralyzed brother in the house. And while tunneling, one of his own burglar booby-traps killed him. Sad and nutty stuff! They both died in the house and became rat food until their remains were discovered by workmen when Police had them remove about one hundred and thirty tons of garbage from their place. And back then, the estate was worth about one hundred grand or in today's money, one and one half-million. Who knows, she may have been related to the Collyer family without knowing it! I think a lot of people are. They suffer from Acute Clutteritis. Those be my words. How about another: Clutterist! That's what she is, Ms. Gretchen Collins, a Clutterist! And I don't think she likes Tamara too much if any at all. Why? Because she sold a bunch of girlie magazines to Hotalova when he saw them in her shopping cart and said they were collector's items. After seeing she got a few bucks from him, she would go up to his apartment door and hand them to Tamara, who just about dropped dead even when holding them with thumb and middle finger. Tamara later blew her stack at Gretchen, especially when the woman asked her for a dollar a magazine. I remember the noise in the hall that day, and when Hotalova came home from work. Then it really hit the fan! Poor Gretchen. All she was doing was performing a public service to make a porno-addict happy!

Porno-addiction is a disease, yes? No? Why not? Every other habit these days is a disease! How do you expect the drug companies to get motivated to find a cure, a magic pill to treat the thing? Can you visualize it? 'Porngobye' Capsules, 100 milligrams. "Oh Hotalova, it's time for your medicine, open the door please?" says Tamara, and the Hotski replies, "Okay Tam, give me a few more minutes to finish the magazine. Do you realize 'Porngobye' is working? Remember how I used to need two hours to finish the magazine? These pills are great for speedreading! And now I do the tapes and DVD's in one-fifth of the time I used to!"

Ah Gretchen, look what happens because you didn't have any holy magazines for Tamara! So, after that she told Hotalova he'd have to come down to her door if he wanted more collector's items. I know that didn't bother him at all, but after a while the business arrangement stopped because Gretchen said she didn't like the way he was looking at her. I think she told that to Tamara who told her to take Hotalova on her collection routes so they could do their buyer/seller stuff away from the building. Can't say I blame her. How about you? This is not how neighbees are supposed to be. We're supposed to be like clumps of wet and dry leaves stuck together on the drainholes of the steel sewer grate at the end of the curb gutter in the street. Listen, don't take sides. First, hear how they became mortal enemies. I call it "Pantygate", you know, like "Watergate" with President Nixon? Why "Pantygate"? I figured you'd ask, but this kind of stuff shows you how the mind gets unhinged when somebody lives an out-of-bounds life. I'm talking about the Hotski, not the Holyski--am I ringing your bells or not?

Now, I don't know, you have to draw your own conclusions, but I'll just try to help you make the connections, okay? I got this from a neighbee who shall remain nameless unless he surfaces in another chapter. I think Madame Backissue missed the dealing with Hotalova and--I don't know, maybe she's a sentimental clutterist, seeing that she seems to like holding on to everything else in print, that is, who knows what else? Here's the deal: It is Valentine's Day. This neighbee lives on the fourth floor and when he entered the stairway to go down, who's coming up but Madame Backissue huffing and puffing. She stops midway between floors on the landing, and has a stack of magazines about a foot and a half high. Do you need to guess what kind they are? The top one was Hustler magazine, but it was with the back cover on top. Now, I didn't ask the neighbee how he knew it was a Hustler, but figured he must know his back covers. So, he sees the woman is about to drop dead and asks if he can carry them for her. She thanks him and tells him where to put them on the fifth floor. Once he hears it's the Yestadey apartment, maybe that's how he made the Hustler connection--what else could Hotalova be reading? This is Yestadey's news! Up the stairs he goes, leaves them right in front of the Yestadey apartment door, and comes back down the stairs. Madame Backissue thanks him again and he goes back down on his way.

Unfortunately, the same day, Neighbee Tamara takes a trip over the pile of porno print, suffers a bone bruise on her right elbow and pulls out her back, for I think about two weeks--I don't know what else. So, there she was, out of commission, and of course, so was Hotalova, but not just because of that, bad as it was. You see, when she tripped and the magazines went flying and sliding, what also was exposed was a pair of dirty bloomers! These probably were either from Gretchen's laundry to do, or possibly were there folded in when she picked up the magazines on her route. Anyway, I heard she went ape, you know, like turned into a wild female gorilla with a grudge--who wants to be near that? Hotalova comes home and gets an earful--probably both ears. He is baffled. A couch full of his sextbooks (that's right, the "t" belongs there), and a pair of dirty bloomers stuck to the couch doily where he parks his head every night, and they don't look anything like the ones worn by Tamara back in the days when he knew what they looked like. Then, Tamara shows up in an arm sling and ba-boom! So, that's Pantygate!

I heard from somebody else, you know, the grapevine? Yeah, there's one here, but some of this stuff I hear is so old it's like raisins instead. Oh yeah, now what did I hear? That he got Madame Backissue a Valentine's Day card the day after, and slid it under her door with some cash and the panties in a manila envelope. What I don't know is if Gretchen got burned because she meant the rag-mags to be a Valentine's gift for filthy Hotalova, or if the money wasn't enough or that the panties had been a gift for him also--why ruin them by washing? Or, that he didn't knock so she could see him face to face and not like the way he would look at her, if you follow my bouncing ball. Or, that he was afraid to knock and risk a floor-to-ceiling column of magazines falling on both of them and burying them at the door, stuck together like a clump of wet and dry leaves on the drainholes of the steel sewer grate at the end of the curb gutter in the street.

It is not my place to know these things, unless I am called to act in love, courtesy, and respect, not as the NYPD who does Professionalism instead of love, but courtesy first, because it is CPR, whereas neighbees is CLR, to be CLeaR. They have to, and we have to. By the way, when they go home, they are somebody's neighbees too.

If You're Going
To Put Words
In My Mouth
You may as well
Include The Toll!

Love your
neighbor MY
way or The
HighWay!
Post-Modern
BiBle CoaLition
Society

Lauria

Where Tamara Yestadey Becomes To Me Yesterday But Not X-ed Out Completely On My Calendar

Now here's where Tamara pulls away from the pack as a neighbee. She's down in my place with the front door open, all the window shades up, having lunch with me before she goes to some prayer meeting. She tells me the man who wants to marry her must love Jesus the way she does, and be willing to marry a woman who is a "porn-widow" even though we're really talking about a divorcee, if she is already or when she is one. So, I asked, "What about someone who just wants to be your neighbee? You know, like Mr. Rogers on the kids TV program, remember him?" She tells me that's okay, if such people still exist. I asked, "What about me? I still exist!" She comes back with, "Does that mean you're not interested in me as a possible spouse?" I said, "I don't think of women that way." Her comeback was predictable: "Well, in what way then are you interested?" And I said, "For now, just as a neighbee. Doesn't the Bible say to love your neighbee? It doesn't say go to bed with your neighbee! So, for now, I'm just interested in loving my neighbees.." "That's good, Stinko, I can live with that as long as you don't make any false moves." she replies. "Listen Tamara", I told her, "False people make false moves. I believe neighbees should be fast friends, like clumps of wet and dry leaves stuck together on the drainholes of the steel sewer grate at the end of the curb gutter in the street. If one leaf wet or dry happens to lay on top of another, well, they're in the gutter, and that's what happens. We can't control what goes on in the gutter." That got her. "Hold on now, Stinko," she says, "there's a little clause in there I don't think I heard before. What's this stuff about the leaves laying on top of one another? Now you have me thinking! All that time you spend on the stoop with Drinkie, is that a 'leaf-lay' scenario? Do you mean to tell me you and she are not having leaf-connection activities? How closely are your wet and dry leaves connecting there?"

That was it. I told her, "Tamara, I realize because you lived with Hotalova and saw the way he thought and looked at all those dirty movies and magazines, and God knows what else, it gives you trust problems. But that was Yestadey and yesterday, but today is not that, Tamara, because Yestadey is not here today, and you're really 'Sleighme', maiden name 'Sleighme', not Yestadey 'slimey', got it? Good! I knew you'd get my subtle word play there." Then she hits back my serve: "And what about that funny look in her eyes, Stink?" Score! I return with "Tamara, if you mean that sky-blue right one with the hot raised eyebrow, not the greenish-brown left one with which she winks at policemen, firemen, and mail-carriers wearing shorts, who have nice knees, that's just a look, I don't know what's in her head--I can only go by what I've seen and done with her all these years. The only thing a little off with her has to do with an agreement Fulmuna and Boobie have with one another."

Now her eyes light up: "Oh, don't tell me. I think I know what's coming, unless there's something even dirtier in the wash!" She caught me by surprise, so I asked "What do you know, Tam?" "I see them," she says, "Fulmuna on the roof and Boobie the boob from his window. Is that the agreement, to spy on one another's wife?" "So, you know!" I said, "But they wear bathing suits!" That got her going, "Bathing suits! What's the difference, Stinko? It's still sick! The Bible calls that the lust of the eyes, don't you get it? Those guys are on the verge of wife-swapping!" I nodded, what could I say? "Yeah, Tam, I guess it's not normal." And she jumped in like a French swordsman in the 17th century, to pierce the word "Normal" as if in the balloon over my head if we were comic book characters-- how's that for imagery?—"What is 'normal', Stinko, is that everything is sin! Sin! Sin! No matter what you hear, what you see, it's all sin, sin, sin!"

And hearing her go into a momentary religious rave, if you know what I mean, reminded me of a concert about seventy years ago before I was born, with Benny Goodman, a great clarinetist, and Gene Krupa, a great drummer, and it was called "Sing, Sing, Sing". And in my head where all the movies of the future play, I did not see a Tamara Yestadey in my marriage future. I mean, maybe others in her church are different than she is, I don't know, I'd have to check them out--and then she interrupted my movie with "And I heard Drinkie say more than once about you and her, that you're the man and she's the woman, and they be our neighbees all around us. Now, what is that supposed to mean, Stinko? It sounds very intimate. Shouldn't she reserve that comment for Fulmuna?" So, I answered, "Why not ask her, maybe she does, or maybe calls him something else, like 'Ful, you're the husband and I'm the wife!' But to me Fulmuna is the man married to the woman and I'm another man who loves the woman as neighbees should like clumps of wet and--" "Okay, okay," she interrupts, "I know all about the sewer stuff!" So, we left things as they were: Me the man, Drinkie the woman, and Tamara the Yestadey, who would likely be "Yesterday", spelled the other way, today and likely tomorrow and tomorrow and tomorrow.

Chapter Six

The Doombrowski's

Meet Cliff and Edna Dombrowski. This should really have been the last chapter if I were to go by the way these people think and even with the hint I see in their names: add an "o" to the last one revealing "Doom"! Then, his first name, like something you can fall off or jump from: Eeeeaaaaaaahhh! And "Edna": remove the "a", do a little word jumble and bingo! It's the "End"!

For the Doombrowski's, the end is near, and these are not Bible believers, but rather, "Liable believers"! That is, as long as there's a chance something bad can happen, forget about the odds against it, it's DOOM! Am I connecting here or what? Are you reading the tea leaves or the coffee grinds, or even the tea bag? In their apartment, they make room for DOOM!

This is not unusual. We had two Presidents, the 19th and 23rd ones, President Hayes and President Harrison about whom J. J. Lauria wrote in his book "All About The Presidents Or Foibles Ole Aesop Would Have Loved To Write", were allegedly said to be big on Doombrowski-like fears. So, you see, you don't have to be President to be blessed with irrational fears. They can save your life. It's pretty safe under your bed during the next eclipse, if you get my drift. That is, unless 450 pound "Trampolina" is doing her aerobics on the mattress, which in itself is not recommended during an eclipse, and besides, how did she get into the apartment? But let's leave that and concentrate now on what makes the Doombrowski's tick, before the clock stops and like wet and dry leaves we clump together on the drainholes of the steel sewer grate at the end of the curb gutter in the street which won't be too bad as long as Doombrowski-like fears don't unsettle us enough to go down the drain--perish the thought!

The couple has five locks on their apartment door and told Drinkie that the Landlord is a fool for not having flood and earthquake insurance even though neither damaging event has happened in this vicinity in recorded history. So of course we're all fool-neighbees because I don't think anyone else in the building has such coverage either. Maybe after a few "just because it never happened doesn't mean it couldn't" sessions with the Doomski's, they might have some company. And, they make their case so believable. Drinkie told Edna that Lloyd's of London would be glad to insure her against rape by Martians, and she didn't take that too well for some strange reason, even though the premium is probably less than five dollars a year if you can be included in a group plan. Martian rape is nothing to scoff at. I'm tempted to disguise my voice and call her as an agent of the MRI Company. This stands for "Martian Rape Insurance". Of course I'll say I'm a local agent because direct calls from the Red Planet are very expensive, if you get my outer space drift, are we connecting here or what?

These neighbees don't consider me much of a neighbee, and told on me to Tamara who then told on her--Edna, that is, or should I change that to "Enda" to describe her better?--to me. Are you confused yet? Don't blame you, let me tell you what put me on the "Shot list". Ahah! Thought I was going to say something else, huh? Well, it's "Shot" because my relationship to the Dooooombrowski's is shot! What am I supposed to do when somebody wastes my time with their stupid fear because they won't let it go nor remove the condition?

Here's the scoop: I'm in the tub one night, and no, not worrying about Fulmuna or Boobie with their binocular games because I don't have anything to offer their hungry, lustful eyes. So, Drinkie comes in, because I don't lock the door so if anything happens to me, even though nothing will as far as I'm concerned, she can just check in on me, especially when I take a nice hot bath and am liable to sink in sleep like a submarine and drown, so I usually call her or Fulmuna when I'm ready for a bath, to check on me--not Tamara, because she'll think I'm playing lust games with her, and is real holy anyway, and forget about Hotalova whose mind needs a bath, and not Isabella because Boobie would never be convinced I'm not out to play the same with her, and he won't check up on me because he says real men don't take baths, they take showers! Isabella laughed at him when she heard it on the stoop--where else?--and snapped back with "Real men don't take a one-minute shower, either!" And right away I could tell he's jealous because Isabella seems to always find a way of defending me and turning it into an opportunity to give him a dig--get the picture? Am I cooking spaghetti here or what?

Now, where was I? Oh yeah, in the tub, and the phone rings, and who had a cellphone back then--and that wasn't too long ago! There I go, disturbing myself because I thought it might be important, and I get out of the tub and trail suds and water to the hall by the kitchen and grab the wall phone which was still ringing, and who is it? It's "Enda"--you guessed it, right? "Stinko, Stinko! Please, I need your help, we're gonna die up here! Please come, can you come? will you? please!" I asked her what it was and she tells me it's gas. So I told her to stay still and not touch anything and I'll be right up. I threw on my robe and went up to her place. She opens the door with a look of panic on her face. It was gas but faint, so I go to her kitchen stove and there is a pot with soggy spaghetti in the water, and the gas jet is on but there is no flame because the pot boiled over and the hot water bubbles put out the flame. So I turned off the jet and said "Here's your problem, Enda, the flame was put out by the boiling pot!" She waves a finger at me, "You shouldn't come here dressed like that!" "But you called me saying you're dying!" I answered. "Yes," she says, "but you could catch pneumonia, you're all soaking wet and that thin robe is wet and you're ruining my linoleum squares, they're going to come up!"

Now I can't talk, my mind wants to curse, my wet feet want to run, and my hands, well, let's forget about them, so I asked, "I'm sorry, Enda--" " 'Edna!' That's the second time you called me that!" she scolded. Holding back my anger, I snapped, "Where's the Cliff-hanger?" "What's wrong with you, Stinko, calling us all these names? I'm afraid people who hear you are going to get our names wrong also, and then we'll wear ourselves out correcting them! Why should we get sick over that? There's enough to worry about!" "Yes, Mrs. Doombrowski, you said it!" I answered. In a flash, the correction came from under the day bed in their living room: "Dombrowski, Mr. OIe! Like in "Bomb, not Boomb!" It was Cliff-o! "And what are you doing under there, Cliff?" I asked. "What was I supposed to do, Mr. Ole, get blown up?" he asked, like I don't know what the story was. So, my logic kicked in, "And what about your wife? What about her getting blown up?" "Someone had to make the call, and she was more frightened than I was so she made it!" he said, from his safe haven. "Well, that was good thinking, Cliff-o. You were the brave one under the day bed, so you stayed under there to protect the day bed in case the apartment blew up. There's got to be some kind of medal for bravery in such a case!" I said, getting real sarcastic as I processed the heroic Doombrowski's reasoning. "Besides," he said, "if she got badly injured, at least I'd be there to care for her!" That short-circuited my smart-box! He had taken us to a new level: self-sacrifice! I just about had it and was getting a little chilled while hot under the collar, if you can catch my Kodak moment with this pair. "Well, I'll sound the 'All Clear' signal so you can come out from under the bed, Mr. D" I told him. "But I still smell gas, Mr. Ole, what should I do?" he pleaded. "Come out, I think it's your own gas, this has been a trying time for you, Mr. D." I said, marveling at my own patience. "I don't think it's mine, Mr. Ole, I know the difference!" he said with a tone of annoyance that I should get so personal. Then he put the knife in: "And your name is 'Stinko', not mine!" "Clifford!" Edna barked in obvious displeasure.

" 'Rostinko' is my proper name, 'Rostinko', Mr. D." I said gently. "Oh, but what are we to do, Stinko, what to do?" 'Enda' begged, "This is serious stuff!" "That it is, dear neighbee, and if I were you, I'd strain the soggy spaghetti before it turns into a flavorless casserole. Food safety also counts!" I said, as if doing a commercial for Good Housekeeping magazine. Then I made my way back down to the bathroom, got back in the tub, still luke-warm, turned on the hot water tap and continued my fearless bath. Fearless, that is, except for ensuring Drinkie would make sure I no doze and drown after drinkie-ing the bathwater!

I could tell you other things about these fear-filled neighbees, but my fear would then be that their fear becomes your fear, and that would not be fair, it would be fear, I'm afraid. Am I making myself clear? Watch your macaroni pot. Who wants to eat pasta that is clumped together like wet and dry leaves........oh, you know what else goes with that. And by the way, do you see how good it is to have neighbees who practice Courtesy, Love, and Respect for one another? If they don't, then you have to call in the Community parents, that's right! Boy! You're getting quick: Momma and Pappa NYPD, who do Courtesy, Professionalism, and Respect. That's why we pay big taxes. You see, if we all did the neighbees thing, the NYPD could go home and enjoy their own neighbees thing: Courtesy, Love, and Respect. Is that CLeaR? Almost.

CHAPTER SEVEN

Oh, And Also Beware Of Dirty-Minded Boobies

Hi again, Neighbee! You ever hear people say the same thing over and over? I do, and it's mostly myself, but I don't get bored because usually I say interesting things before or after that--you know what I mean, do you get the picture? I won't wait for an answer--I know we're connecting, right? So, listen to this: Boobie sits down on the stoop a few days ago and tells me this startling bit of confidentiality: "Stinko, you're the man!" Which of course I already knew, then he throws in, "I gotta apologize to you!" "What for, Boobie?" I asked. Then he gets real personal: "I thought you were looking to score with Isabella, but now I see you differently. Drinkie always says about you that you're the man, and she's the woman, and everybody else around is the neighbees, and even though it sounds like you and she are 'fornicating'--like Holy Tamara called it when she was telling Isabella about Hotalova and his movies and magazines, I see that you and the Drink are more like brother and sister and I'm sort of ashamed for what me and Fulmuna are doing." Baboom! That hit me like a ton of bricks! Make it two tons, maybe three! Could it be Tamara is doing the prayer-thing on these guys, or at least this one? I didn't know. I couldn't believe she got to the Boob directly or Isabella, but then again, I just didn't know.

Then he gives me the lowdown, and I got the picture clear: "Y'know, I'm not a good Catholic, but the other night I ran into Father Rutuolo while walking home, and so I asked him what he thought about two

35

broads checking out each other's husband in the shower with the husbands knowing about it." "Wow!" I let out, "Who'd ever think of getting a church-take that way on what you guys are doing? Very sharp, Boobie!" So he says more: "And listen to his call, Stinko. He says it sounds to him more a case of those broads being pimped out by their husbands!" "He said 'Broads'?" I asked. "Yeah, Stinko, like with a capital B R O A D S!" he shoots off, like I was the one he was worked up about. "Y'know, I never thought about it that way. So, I said 'Father, couldn't we say they're just peeping them out?' Then get this, Stink: 'Peeping, pimping, same sin my son. You're all going to hell, all four of you!' 'Whoa! Wait a sec, Father!' I told him, 'That's not me, I'm just posing a scenario, please!' So, he looks at me with that holy fish eye. I know that look, seen it before, and he says: 'I'm not accusing you, Boobie, it's just a way of speaking, but the four of you are going to hell, anyway! I don't know what you're doing, but even thinking about this kind of trash is sin! Oh, and if you see Tamara Yestadey tomorrow, tell her I said I missed hearing her confession last week, but I'll be calling her.' And guess what, Stink? He still had the holy fish eye on me. He knew something. I'd stake your life on it!" "My life!" I jumped in. "Why my life? I'm not gonna gamble with that!" "Okay, okay, Stink," he says, "Drinkie's life! Happy?" I sort of was, but now he had Drinkie on the gambling block, anybody but himself! So on he goes: "And you know how I knew, Stinko? Can you dope it out, read the tea leaves?" Enough, I thought, his mind is going, but then again, maybe not! "No, Boob," I said, "I'm in a state of suspended fascination! Educate me!" "This was it, Stinko, he says, 'and say hello to Stinko for me--that guy should have become a priest. And also make sure Isabella prays for a spiritual cleansing as well as a physical one when she showers tonight!' Now what the hell is that supposed to mean? He's good Stinko, the man is good, and I'm feeling more like a freakin' pimp on the hour since then--I hardly slept today and don't like the idea of going to hell because of a bathing beauty mutual appreciation contest!"

"Boobie," I tell him, "I think Tamara is feeding him, you know what I mean--get my drift?" "Feeding?" he asks, "You mean like finking on us? The bitch! I thought the confession booth was for confessing your own sins, not somebody else's!" Then I had to be real creative, so I said "Boobie, you make all the sense in this screwed up world--and that's saying something, but maybe she said something and he took it to another level, like the choir loft." "Yeah, choir loft, my bony buttocks! How about the cellar where he probably keeps all the ceremonial wine?" he steams. "No, no!"

I said, "Although, that could be too; you might have a point there, like the steeple where the belfry is. How about, she says to him, 'Father I must confess when I see a neighbee like Fulmuna on the roof with spyglasses, and then another night, my other neighbee Boobie with spyglasses, I start thinking they're looking at each other's wives in the shower, even though their wives wear bathing suits there! So, forgive me for maybe judging them the wrong way.'?"

"No way, cockroach!" he snaps--giving me a new title, leave it to the Boob! Some nerve! He had them too! Hey, we live in an apartment building. Everybody's got them, or better maybe to say they has us. I know it's "have", but "has" makes the point, right? And really, I should have said I don't like being called that. I prefer "cockaroach". That "a" makes a big difference to me--don't ask why. Anyway that's my take on this. "You're cutting them too much slack," says the Boob, "I don't damn freakin' need her to confess the sins of her neighbees on all these floors, especially when I'm one of the sinners if you want to call admiring another woman than my wife, a sin! Aren't we supposed to love our neighbees, not rat them out? She's a fink! Maybe she's the one going to hell!" So, now he gets me crazy with scenarios, you know what I'm trying to say? Can you connect the dots? So, I hit him with the kind of stuff that Hotalova used to drool about: "Look, Boobie, aside from my liking Tamara even though she's a bit overboard with the religious stuff—". "I know," he interrupted, "you two are fast friends, like a clump of wet and dry leaves--" "No, no," I stopped him, having an idea of his next several words, "imagine me doing with Isabella what Hotalova looked at in his lust-pile--?" "Ahah! I knew it!" he snarled, "You're not satisfied clumping Tamara, now you want to really steam up the leaves! I thought I knew you better than that! You're 'The man' all right! Wait until Fulmuna hears this! And then Drinkie! I guess the next 'Imagine' will be about you and Drinkie clutching each other's hardware on the drainholes of the steel sewer grate at the end of the curb gutter in the street--yeah!--and make it a rainy day so you'll be doing it like the beach scene in 'From Here To Eternity!' An Oscar-winning performance, roach-man!"

Too much, I couldn't take it anymore, so I nailed him: "Okay, Boobie, that's it! You are going to hell! You! And more than Father Rutuolo spelled out, but I'm going to Heaven with Tamara, and maybe Drinkie, and maybe even Isabella, and none of us are taking our bathing suits with us!" With that, he really blew a fuse: "Put up your hands, you F-ing piece of slime, go ahead!" "No, Boobie, I'll let you pound on me so I'll be absolutely sure you're going to hell, hitting a defenseless neighbee! Screw you! My motto hasn't changed, it's still 'Courtesy, Love, and Respect', like the NYPD except--" "I know, you son of a--" he interrupted, then I cut him off before he turned my mother over in her grave, although I think she checked out of there before they did her up at the Funeral home, but it's just a way of talking, you get my drift, yes? Good. So, I added "That's right, Boob-O, except they do Professionalism!"

Then he really mushroomed, "Put up your hands, you _____[this one I couldn't even give a hint on]!" "Sorry, Boobhead, I'd rather let you do the assault so the law will be on my side. Shame on you! Grow up and keep your dirty suspicions to yourself. For you it's hell, baby, I mean Boobie, and I'm going to Heaven with the girls and no bathing suits!" With that he stomped away like he was talking to himself like a raving cellphone user, you know what I'm saying?

Meanwhile, I felt good about helping the priest with my call, or should I say, Boobie's sentence--good, right? So, don't agree, you're going to hell, too. And I also felt closer to Tamara, but not to clump her like dirty Boobie was talking. Actually, I felt sort of clean, you get it? Am I scoring with your mind? It just don't get any better--not better, no way Hose-ay!

Oh, and by the way, I can confess to you, not Father Rutuolo--who's liable to tell me to go to hell or that I'm going there, you never know-- that I don't know if the Boob-head is Bipolar or Paranoid or a Schizo. Hey, and this makes me crazy also. Being English-second-language, who can understand why "Schizo" is really "Skitso"? What's wrong with these people? If I do things their way, then "Stinko" should be "Stincho"! Now I'm getting Bipolar! Anyway, I think I'm gonna save words regarding the Boob by calling him "Schizopolaroid", okay? That'll really make him crazy, which he is, is he not?

Some neighbors smoke too much while others
play Scrabble with clergy in the next room.

CHAPTER EIGHT

Holy Smoke With Scrabble And Sydelle

Hi Readie! Last time I felt clean like this was about a dozen years ago when Morris the Butcher lived next door--remember him? Probably not, but don't let it move your mind off the page. Now look how this goes: Morris was a retired butcher, not a Kosher butcher, but still a good "meat sculptor". Doesn't that sound classier than "Butcher"? And Morris was about eighty, his wife Sydelle, a chain-smoker two years older than him-- probably from smoking. So, I used to go to his apartment every Wednesday night at eight and guess who also came? You'll never--give up now--don't waste your time trying. Father Rutuolo, whose first name is Rudy. That's right, the Priest! Of course he was twelve years younger then but now he's twelve years older. That's what time does, it adds years to your age. Don't take it from me, check it out.

So, why was he there? To play Scrabble! That was it, unless it was a Jewish holiday, or Catholic Holy day of obligation. That was it. We were there to play Scrabble. Sydelle? She was busy in the bedroom with window open, smoking. Yeah, she loved to smoke--Morris didn't. The only time his lungs got that stuff was when he made smoked whitefish. Don't ask me how or what. All I know is he said that was the only smoking he would do. But what about Salmon? Forget it.

And what do you think Sydelle is doing besides puffing her eighty-two year old self to death? She's singing along with Marlene Dietrich records in

German! She looked like her and even sounded like her, and she had this six-inch cigarette holder Morris gave her for her eightieth birthday to help her keep away from cigarettes, at least six inches away, that is, and he had them I think etch or engrave on it, "To Sydelle with love from Marlene."! On her seventy-fifth birthday he gets her an expensive gold cigarette case with diamonds on it, and has it engraved "This is a Mendel case, just like its owner". Get it? How could you, unless you knew their last name was Mendel. Mental or Mendel, no difference as far as it is Sydelle's label. That's the way I see it. Get my drift? Are we cruising on automatic pilot or what?

So get this: Sydelle tells me she used to be a cigarette-girl--you know, the knockout ones who walked around with a tray of all the favorite brands, including cigars, and ugh! Chewing tobacco. I used to see them in old movies. And, one day this guy gives her a stack of Raleigh coupons. You know, each pack of Raleigh cigs had a coupon under its wrap worth about one cent, but you could turn them in for things you could use, like a toaster or spyglasses, whatever.

Well, anyway, Sir Walter Raleigh, or whatever his name was--I call him that because he seemed to have cornered the market on Raleigh coupons, wait 'til you hear!--invites her up to his place to see his coupon collection and things he got for them--he must have been smoking for three hundred years. Had it been four hundred, I'd have suspected him to be Sir Walter himself, who was such a gentleman I recall learning, somewhere in school, that he threw down his cape in the gutter so some fancy dame--that's what they used to call the women in England who reached the level of a Knight: a dame--didn't get mud on her fancy dress.

Dame. Ha! Why not call them a "Day", you know, like "Knight & Day". Doesn't that sound more logical? Of course, because the "K" in Knight is silent, you wouldn't know if "Knight & Day" referred to time or Knighthood, but that could be easily fixed by sounding the "K", like you are talking about a knish, and to make sure people who hear you don't think you're just being crabby, you might add a knish to the conversation after sounding the "K" after mentioning knight, for example, "You know, I think what would show you the difference between a K-night and a gentleman, is that a K-night, at some point in your Konversation will offer you a knish, whether he has one or not."

Now let's not forget about that mud-soaked cape! You see, if they had sewer drains in Jolly ole England back in the days of King James I, maybe there wouldn't have been mud in the gutter, and maybe there wasn't even a gutter! The whole street was a gutter, an utter gutter! So for sure, nothing was going on atop the drainholes of steel sewer grates at the end of the curb gutters in the streets, because there were probably no curbs, no steel sewer grates, and no a lot of other things, except for clumps of wet and dry leaves stuck together or trying to get stuck together--get my drift?--and that's not a dirty drift, because without that clean clumping, you don't have life, just drift, and mud for sure, plenty of it, too. Get it? Good.

You must keep that in mind. Dirty clumping ain't the way to go. Clean clumping makes good things happen and nobody gets hurt. Call it Holy Mattressmony. Why not?

So now, almost four hundred years later, Sydelle the Sigarette Girl (nice title, why not?) is at the coupon-king's apartment. He gives her a Raleigh cigarette and a shot of scotch, and even though she doesn't smoke or drink, she takes them and shortly after, as he tries to make his move-- you knew that was coming, of course--she throws up on his couch! Then, having figured out she's in trouble, duh!, she tells him it's not the cigarette or drink, but pills she takes for Syphilis. With that good news he calls her a cab and stuffs her bag with a fat stack of the coupons. She never sees him again at the club, but that sets her off smoking Raleigh's and collecting coupons 'til they stopped that program whenever that was. The program stopped but the smoking continued, and there you are: "Smokey Sydelle"!

A short while later she meets Morris Mendel at some twenty and over dance party, and bingo! Maybe it was a bingo party? Anyway, there she is, no kids, married a whole bunch of years to a Scrabble addict, the Michaelangelo of The Meat Market!

Meanwhile, Father Rutuolo and Morris were dueling over the alphabet with me, and they were real good at it! There was no time limit on our moves and I never took too long anyway, but they did, so guess what went on--no, don't--you won't get it--listen to this: while Morris is waiting for the Father, he whips out a Bible in Hebrew and is reading the Psalms. While the Priest is waiting, he's got an Italian Bible and is reading also the Psalms! You can't make this stuff up! So, the second time I saw this, I started joking that they were really reading foreign language dictionary pages and cheating. That got them going on me as a heathen, which I'm not, and Morris said I looked like a nice Jewish boy and should be married, and the Priest said I should attend Mass and the Twenty & Over dances in the school gymnasium because the girls out-numbered the guys two to one.

43

Anyway, that's how I found out they were both reading the Psalms, which they told me were the prayers of King David and very good for me to read in English. I'm still thinking about it. Who knows, maybe I will, and not just if I get into big trouble.

Morris would ask me what kind of a name was Ole? Spanish? And I told him just look on the bell down by the entrance--playing games with him. So he did and asks me why I don't use my whole last name, which is Olevenkoskyak. I told him it's thirteen letters last time I counted, and I'm superstitious. So I just blurted out "What if your last name was 'Mendelovoskak'? Would you change it to 'Men'?" Rutuolo, uh, Father Rutuolo, that is, asks, "How do you spell that"? So, I spelled out the letters and they were blown away that it was exactly thirteen letters! "How'd you do that?" the Father asks, "That's sort of miraculous!" Morris then asked, "Are your parents still alive?" "No." I replied. "Anybody in your family Jewish?" he asks. "Maybe, why?" I ask, and he tells me "Because that kind of brilliance comes from a Russian-Jewish mind!" And the Priest then says, "Don't leave out the Italian mind, Morris!" Then Morris continues, "Olevenkoskyak Italian?" "No, Mendelovoskak!" the Father jumps in to answer, "That's not Italian!"

Then Morris seemed to be getting annoyed, I think because he had to go to the bathroom, and think also he was afraid to leave his Scrabble letters unguarded. "Morris, look, I'm saying the fact that Stinko can come up with Mendelovoskak in a split-second is something a brilliant Italian mind is capable of!" Now Mendel is trying to control himself, looking like he's holding in his urgent need to relieve himself. Just then Sydelle comes in saying, "The bowl is stopped up, I hope nobody has to go!" Then Morris says "Stinko, can I go to the bathroom in your apartment?" So, I said "Go ahead, the door's open, just don't trip over the laundry I'm separating, it's all over the floor." "Thanks, I'll be careful not to wet your laundry!", he blurted and zipped out the door and I'm sure zipped again.

I thought that wet laundry stuff a strange answer, but then again, when one has to go, one can say what one wouldn't if they didn't have to, you get what I'm trying to say, yes? That happens a lot with Scrabble players, you know, the Prostrate? If that has only one "r", don't sweat it, you'll still score by putting your Prostrate on the board.

Anyway, Morris made it and when he came in, and Sydelle--who was filling her old Ronson lighter--remember them?--asks me, "What kind of a name is 'Stinko', Stinko?" And I said a little joke: "Those cigs are making you stutter, Sydelle!" Then she stuns me with this one: "Does 'Stinko' have anything to do with hygiene?" So then I really stabbed her--if you know what I'm saying, but only fooling around, you know what I mean--get the picture? I said, "No, Syd, I don't smoke." So she gets a little hot, "Do you notice smoke on me?" Then I hit her big, "Sydelle, I can't tell because the whole apartment smells like a gypsy cab even though everything is in order, and I'm sure it's on my clothes and in my hair--that's the way it goes with smokers."

"Okay, okay, I must give you an 'A' for honesty." she says, calming way down. Meanwhile, Father Rutuolo and Morris are settled there in suspended fascination. Then Morris asks me, "Is 'Stinko' short for 'Rostinko'?" "Yes!" I said, "How did you guess?" And watch this. What do you think he tells me, and us, that is? Forget it--you'll never guess. I'll tell you. "It's the Jewish mind!" And with that we all laughed and went on Scrabbling, and Sydelle? Well, she lit up again and went back into her tobacco den. You know, I got a Passover card from them a few months ago. Can you imagine? And in it he says they're doing fine in Boca Raton. They're in their nineties and she's cut down to four packs a day because the doctor said if she doesn't cut down, she might need a lot of Raleigh coupons to get a lung transplant when she reaches one hundred. Don't you wonder how I can remember just about word for word what we all said back then? Well, don't. I'll tell you: It's my brilliant Russian, Jewish, and Italian mind. I really miss them. I'm sure Father Rutuolo does too, they were good neighbees, and we were fast friends, like clumps of wet and dry leaves stuck together on the drainholes of the steel sewer grate at the end of the curb gutter in the street.

You know where I got that string of words about neighbees being clumps? Sydelle. That's right--it was from her-- I never forgot it. I'd probably forget it, but in my head is a picture of those wet and dry leaves stuck together on the drainholes, and guess what's stuck there also to the clump?--no, forget it, you'll never get it: a crumpled up empty pack of Raleigh cigarettes with no coupon--that's Sydelle's. She'll never go down the drain in my mind. She's part of the clump even in Boca Raton, which incidentally, in Spanish means "Rat mouth". So there you go, "Butt mouth" lives in "Rat mouth", a real long-distance clump, hah?

CHAPTER NINE

Chief Orville Late-Lee Earlie Speak Wisdom

"White Man took our lands, killed our Buffalo, poisoned our lakes, streams, rivers. He one bad injun! Why now I trust him?"

With these 22 words, Neighbee Orville, or as Fulmuna affectionally calls him, "The Chief", separated himself from everyone who wasn't a South-of-the-border or North-of-the-border Western Hemispherian--my words, not his.

And who could blame him? You didn't think I could speak this high-English, did you? Admit it! Well, I can. And how do you like the word "Mantra"? Yes, that's what my definition or analogy or label is for the Chief's 22-word complaint.

(the "anal" in analogy has nothing to do with the study of man's "south of the border" exit, it just means comparing one thing with another by using an illustration--get my drift? Are we talking turkey here or what? Don't wait for Thanksgiving. That should be everyday)

Well, that is his mantra, just like mine is about wet and dry leaves clumped together..........oh, you know how it goes, right?

I think a mantra is a word or expression that would bring peace. But when you think of that bitter-sounding 22-word history of the European "intrusion",

(note how I zap you with one refined word after another--I'm beginning to like doing this--it also helps me say what I mean the right way and in less words--do you catch my butterflies or is your net broken again?)

it sounds more like a war cry! But the one big big difference between Orville's mantra and mine is that he doesn't realize we're all going down the drain unless we clump together. He's still hung up on settling the score for what somebody else's ancestors did, not mine. But that doesn't make mine any better. I am still Stinko although Orville says my name is wrong and that everybody who like seeing Cowboy and Indian movies where injun is made bad man, they are "Stinko" people, not me. He also feel Indian Casino people should share more of wampum profits with poor Indian and he doesn't trust those owners either--think maybe they are really Italians who just played Indians in movie, because real Indians would help fellow brave when Buffalo chips down.....a little Casino talk connection here--are you catching the native American brilliance? Yes?

I told him we can't solve everybody else's problems and it would be better just to give one homeless-looking person a bag of Buffalo wings with some hot sauce once a week, and keep moving so they don't make a reservation outside your door. I think that one got him to make an "open door" policy as a good neighbee, but stay away from becoming a Buffalo wings-on-wheels distributor who might be followed home like a stray cat might try to do.

We had that Casino talk shortly after I got to know him. About three days later, I'm going upstairs to put a Japanese food menu under Tamara's door--that's a story for another day, maybe half another book, I think-- don't get me going on that one! Anyway, I hear chanting with drums in the background, not loud, just enough to let you know the natives are restless tonight, even though it was still afternoon; and sure enough, it's coming from 2A! The door to the Chief's place is open, so not having seen his pad since he moved in, I pass by and hear the chanting coming from his bathroom where the door is half open. There's running water, and I don't mean the name of an Indian brave. I'm thinking maybe he's shaving with a tomahawk or showering like he's under a small waterfall in the Northern Adirondack woods. You see, my imagination is kicking in and maybe he has just performed an "analogy" and is flushing. Are you following the trail? Good. It's not a cd I'm hearing or a radio--it's him, Late-Lee Earlie, in the shower and chanting and drumming on something, I think the tiled wall: "Ya ya wa roombo magondaaaaaa .....hob hob moteetee lafa gongggggggg" over and over again. So I'm thinking Grandpa Bert is gonna have a leak to fix with all this vibration going on, and maybe Helga and her niece Vera in 1A who live right under, will be blessed with the results of this raindance. "Ya ya wa room bo magondaaaaaa.....hob hob moteetee lafa gongggggg", again and again. That was it, I knocked on the steel apartment door jamb, and with the same beat and melody, chanted, "Hiya Chiefo, it's the Stinko, come to see you in the pink-o--", and suddenly he yells, "Stinko? You here Stinko?" And I answered "Yeah, it's me Late-Lee, how you drumming them?" "Ah, my Stinko, great Stinko! That's what I call you now!" he bellows, "The Great Stinko! And you are! You do for me what nobody else do!", patting his face with a bathtowel, his shoulder-length jet-black hair in need of a hairdryer, and wearing a pair of Speedo swim trunks! That hit me like a ton of Buffalo chips, if you get my grazing connection. Not what he said, but the swim trunks! I noticed his bathroom window was not clear glass, so didn't think that somehow he's got some screwy "peepo" deal with Godknowswho. "Hey, uh, Chief! You always shower wearing those?" I asked. He then laughed, answering, "No, Stinko, only to wash them, kill two birds, as you say." Well, that was that, and I started wondering how many other birds he kills if he does the rest of his laundry that way.

"What are you saying about 'The Great Stinko', Chief?" I asked, noticing he looked more on the peacepath than the warpath. Then he reminded me of what I told him about helping just one needy person: "I meet her yesterday, Stinko! She very nice and very needy, but also very helpful! She know things about my future I do not know!"

Oh, oh, I thought, and suddenly got the picture of Salvina, a gypsy woman, who also has an open-door policy, if you catch my flaming Frisbee--don't make me draw pictures for you. She has a storefront apartment on Fielding avenue and a sign in the window: "Tarot card-reading, Health consultations, Bump, Palm, and Foot-reading". Sorry I had to let him down, so I thought: "Yeah, Chief, you met Salvina. But I could be wrong." "No, Salvina her name! She wear sheets like silk, with many colors, and these do not cover her chests too well. I notice this when she read my foot, and sight made reading very happy time!"

Now he had me real curious: "Oh, I'm sure," I said, "and how did the reading go?" His eyes lit up like he was dying to tell me: "Ah, very good reading, my Stinko! I lay on her couch, she hold foot in the air with heel between her chests, and told me I have very good flat feet, but they are lonely feet, like feet that have also been left flat. What she mean by that, Stinko?"

"Um, that means somebody who a person left by surprise or not, but should not have." This was the best I could do, and he caught it. How did I know? He gave me his mantra in shorthand: "Aha, like White man!" Somehow, I knew what was going to heal the Chief's "lonely foot" disease, at least for as long as his wampum lasted: "So, how much for the foot-reading?" I asked. Late-Lee Earlie shook his head: "Don't know. Before I ask, she say 'Give me what you want. My two little ones had breakfast, they can wait for tomorrow to have a little lunch.' That made my heart heavy so I give her seventy dollars--all I have in pouch." "Seventy dollars! For one foot?" I said, almost losing my balance, standing on two. "That is much wampum!"

Then, with a smile as big as a slice of cantaloupe, he explains: "Aha, I see you know Indian words! Yes, my Stinko, but listen to this: as soon as she take money, she roll it up and stuff it between her two chests, and almost lost her standing like you just now, and began howling like coyote, grab my hands, so close I smell she ate garlic something, so I guess today her day to eat lunch. She look eye to eye with me, then say, 'I see she-bear with two cubs come to your cave very soon to make you happy not only on one foot but all over!' Stinko, I hear this, it make me very happy, and better news also--that she is Chippewa squaw-widow!"

Oh, oh, just as I thought. He got sucked in. I just had to tell him: "Chief, Chief, listen to me. I see this woman just about every time I go up the block. She's a gypsy. That means someone from Europe, not an American native. The only thing Chippewa about her is that she wants to chip away at your wallet!" With that, he wrinkles up his already sun-fried, wrinkled face, lowers his head and shakes it in denial: "Ah, no my Stinko, we must not shoot arrow in woods before seeing Moose!" I knew he was getting moosed already and was not going to be out of the woods for a while, if you can catch my camping language. Now this begins to stir my pot, so I change speeds: "Orville, my dear neighbee, and that is spelled 'd e a r', are you planning to move your tent to a bear cave somewhere else or do you not catch she is telling you she's making the clumpity clumpity move on you?"

Shaking wrinkledheadface again, Chief say, "Clumpity, clumpity? You speak like wild horse with no horseshoe! She say she Chippewa!" Now I'm knocking heads with a wooden cigar store indian, and ready to give up, but suddenly, like a bolt of lightning I get zapped with this mindset: "Say Chief, a few minutes ago I think I heard you chanting in Chippewa right here. Am I lying or what?" Late-Lee Earlie straightens up, then stares down at me with a vacant look as if he's somewhere else. He raises both hands like Superman ready to go up for a stratocruise above the clouds, "Stinko, my neighbee-manbrother, those are words to Great Spirit that I say before going to meet Salvina-squaw for more footwork."

I couldn't resist: "Yeah, fancy footwork, all right!" "My Stinko," he replies softly, "the words I spoke were in hope for joining with daughter of my fathers. Who knows if we make tribe increase?" This he says, showing me I can't convince him no matter what, but I got a brainstorm, and threw it at him before he could open his umbrella: "So, Late-Lee, if you chant and she doesn't understand the words, what then? Doesn't that prove she's not Chippewa?" But out of nowhere he whips out the umbrella: "No, dear Stinko, only that she may be of low washerwoman class because of White man. That class cannot gossip with tongue as loose as oak leaf flapping in wind, because they raised in White man house as slave from papoose time and only know White man forked-tongue English." Hearing that, I knew White man could not sit down, pass peacepipe and make Red man see light. Instead, Chief must go for seventy dollars a foot, enjoy life until wake up one day with wallet sprouting buffalo wings and flying away, looking for happier hunting grounds.

Rivers dry up, herds seek other plains, and sometimes squaws find other teepee to tap, if you can read my smoke signals. This would prove not all are neighbees, not all show courtesy, love, and respect, and sometimes that is why we need NYPD come with Courtesy, Professionalism, and Respect, nail the crafty b _ _ _ _, sorry, crafty she-bear (if you fill in blank spaces with "itch", your fault, not mine for saying hard word, ugh!), before Chief Orville Late-Lee Earlie be sucked dry of wampum and go to unhappy hunting grounds with broken heart, broken bank, broken pocket, and no moccasin for flat foot.

By the way, the Chief still lives here, is able to make the rent, but no longer sees Squaw Salvina who seems to be going on with her Chippewa chipping-away on other "Tribesmen". But the Chief and I only exchange nods when we see each other, not even a "How!". I think he got taken bigtime and now considers Squaw Salvina no better than White man, and for some strange reason, me also, and Fulmuna, and Boobie, and my Drinkie, Isabella, and Tamara--let's forget about Hotalova. I also don't know about the other neighbees.

I suspect he think me now real Stinko because I no go to war with him or for him to prevent his getting scalped, if you can catch my Indian warfare message. You close enough to book. No need smoke signal.

Now, he has reservations about me, and those are not Indian, and he cannot clump together like wet and dry leaves stuck on the drainholes of the steel sewer grate at the end of the curb gutter in the street. I don't believe only good neighbee is dead neighbee. Maybe we find way to block sewer. Don't ask "How?" Chief Orville Late-Lee Earlie think you try to say hello, maybe give you nod, maybe grunt, "Ugh!"

By the way, those words to Great Spirit the Chief was chanting, you know, the "magondaaaaaa" stuff? Well, the author who let me narrate "Neighbees" said he'd send its melody notes, you know, a page of sheet music, to anyone who sends him a stamped, self-addressed envelope with a money order made out to him for twenty bucks--to him not me. He says the money will all go to the GCCCLF (Gypsy Chip-a-way Chippewa Children's Lunch Fund). His idea is to take away the excuse that the kids have to wait 'til tomorrow to have lunch. That means less squawndering (yeah, the "w" stays there) by Gypsy Chip-a-way Chippewa squaw. Get it? Got it? Good! Smart move, I do say!

Some Neighbees Teach Women Violinists...

CHAPTER TEN

Of Rats And Women And Flaming Fiddlers

While we're on the subject of God, though maybe we're not, but what with Father Rutuolo sending people to Hell and the Mendels being in Florida and Tamara Yestadey sort of making the holy moves on me, I think, let me tell you about Bela, the Atheist. This was four years ago, maybe. Bela lived on the fifth floor just below the Yestadeys. He taught violin at some big music college in Manhattan. Good at it as anybody I ever heard on radio or TV or even in person when the Parks department has Summer concerts--get the picture? He only lived here about ten months then took a Music Professor job at a college in Tennessee. Bela Maritza– "Hungarian Atheist, The Worst Kind!" he used to say about himself. I wouldn't brag about that, being an atheist also--just kidding, just kidding. And I really don't think he was the worst kind, but I can see saying that gets attention, which is what I think he wanted alot--yes?

Anyway, he was single, who knows maybe how many times diworced, no misspelling there, that's the way he spoke, sometimes making me wonder if he had no teeth, but then when he smiled, it lit up his face, probably the light reflecting off the three gold ones, two upper and one lower. And he was really handsome, trim, salt and pepper wavy hair, about fifty I guess, and that long hair flopped around while he fiddled. Boy! What a sight and what a sound!

Now, let me tell you the Atheist part. This is screwy. First day he moved in, Drinkie and I are on the stoop as usual, and he comes trailing after the moving guys with a big pewter crucifix, says "Hello" to us, I then said "Hi", I think, and I remember Drinkie just nodded. Then he's back a few minutes later with a glass-framed painting about a foot and a half square of Baby Jesus in his Mother's arms. He stops and says "I am Bela Maritza, Hungarian Atheist, The Worst Kind, and Violinist, and you must be my new neighbors, yes?" With that Hungarian accent, I thought I was watching an old movie, so I remember smiling and shaking his hand, and he had a real grip!

Drinkie said, "And I am Drinkie Saluna, I whistle." So with that wiseguy kind of reply I thought for sure, that's the end of our neighborliness, but he then looks her up and down like his eyes were feeling everything he was looking at, and she turns red, and he drops this bomb on her--I'll never forget it: "I like your, how you say, sarcasm? But even more your shape and your face. Perhaps you can visit me when I settle down here, and you whistle, and I take out my violin. I think we can do some good things together, yes?" That was about the size of their talking as I recall. Then he really flipped her out by taking her hand and kissing it, while holding the painting! He notices her ring, and asks, "Ah, is your husband dead?" She stutters, saying "N-no!" And he comes back, asking me, "Are you Mr. Saloonhead?" "Saluna!", snaps Drinkie. I then said, "No, no, just a neighbor, Stinko. Stinko Ole." I remember his smiling and saying "Ho ho, 'Stinkie' and 'Drinkie'! Even your strange names go nice together, but you are not married to each other. Very fine!"

Who talks like that? Well, that was him, and when he went upstairs Drinkie said, "Stinko, I don't care how good he looks, and he does, but he gives me the creeps! I think he's an urban cannibal! 'Is my husband dead?' What's with him?" So that was it, and Drinkie avoided him all the while he lived here, except once again on the stoop--I'll tell you about that, if I remember. How I remember this stuff amazes people, especially me.

One conversation I had with him two months after he arrived, cleared up for me what an atheist would be doing with a painting of Jesus and Mother Mary. I just put it to him straight: "Bela, how come you call yourself a Hungarian Atheist and Violinist, but you have a painting of Baby Jesus and Mother Mary in your pad. What gives?" So, he solves my curiosity with, "Stinkie, my friend, I want to believe. Even with all the Soviets did to my country back in the 1950's, they could not take the Madonna and her holy child out of the hearts of my people, especially the old Magyar mammas. [I later found out Magyar was their way of saying

'Hungarian'] 'Where was God?' so many asked. And I asked too. I still ask. This Jesus and Mother Mary are connected to God big time, as you say here. Well, I keep my painting so people will ask what you asked when they connect my title with the painting. When one of them gives me a good answer for that, I will drop 'Atheist'. Until then I will also play the most beautiful holy music in the world, also to cause them to inquire. Am I saying it right?"

I figured this "urban cannibal" is making a lot of sense, but needed to talk to someone like a Priest or Rabbi who would know where God was then. I would have told him, "Why don't you ask God yourself, Bela?", but I didn't want to stir him up, he seemed to be more serious then than when he moved in, and at any time up to that moment. So, I just said, "Yes, I gotcha, Bela!" And with that he rubbed his hands together and said, "I like your 'gotcha'! It somehow sounds to me like Goulash. Have you ever tasted Goulash?" I had to be honest with him: "Yeah, a few times, and I hated it." "Oh, how unfortunate! I would have taken you to a very fine Hungarian restaurant where I often play when they see me, and ask me to entertain the patrons. Then, what do you know? I eat my Goulash for free! You must come with me sometime. Perhaps bring your Drinkie friend if her husband doesn't mind, and she can whistle while I play. Even if she doesn't whistle, I think we'll all eat for free!" "Sounds good, Bela, we'll see! Thanks!" I said, smiling. And with that we split, and I never took him up on it, being afraid Drinkie might think the Goulash was a cannibal recipe.

Well, anyway, let me tell you where "Atheist" got him thinking, I think, or maybe me and everybody else in the building who caught his act one night, or one early morning I should say. The big pewter crucifix goes up on his living room wall over the expensive leather couch with the big end table next to it, and the Baby Jesus and Mary painting in a frame with glass covering it sitting on the table, and a small cage with a white rat in it with pink eyes. So, Bela, or "Count" Maritza as I used to call him, thinking of Bela Lugosi as Count Dracula in the old horror movies, remember? If not, then you're too young to know and missed all the fun. Nightmare Freddie might've been as scary, but the Count had real class, and would drink your blood. Blah! Scared you a little, didn't I?

Anyway, the Count complains to me about Hotalova in the apartment above his, you know, Tamara's husband? He's got the TV on too loud, and he's watching some porno flick. I said "Bela, use earplugs, like the pig might if you played too loud on the violin. What could he know about great music?" Tamara told me that often, Hotski asked her to sleep using earplugs.

Now, when the Count moved in, he didn't give any lessons there, but about four months before he left, I saw at least three different women come in, at different times with violin cases. Nice looking stuff--no, I'm not talking about the cases--because I was on the stoop with Drinkie, who you must remember said I'm the man, she's the woman, and Fulmuna is the husband, and the rest be our neighbees all around us. So, this goes on a few weeks, and yes, I could hear violin music coming down the courtyard and it's about eleven p.m., then no more violins. About two a.m., the Count comes down and he looks a little, uh, I don't know, maybe it's my imagination, and she also looks, uh, I don't know, again, maybe my imagination, but anyway, a cab pulls up--a few times the cab was already there, motor and I guess meter running, but no beeping at that hour. So, now I'm thinking Porno Hotalova's TV gamma rays are burning holes in the floor right on Bela's head night after night, if you know what I'm trying to say. Then, he's fiddling around with these woman violin players who just didn't look so violinish to me--get the picture?

Kaboom! It happened! I didn't know what, but after midnight, Boobie Slutta is coming up the walk, suddenly a thud, a scream, and a crash in the courtyard! Me and Drinkie run in and see broken glass, a cage with a white rat in it who ain't moving, and up there on the fifth floor looking down, is Bela and this violin woman sort of covered with a sheet, and it was not a sheet of music either, and there is the window next to that one, with no glass in it, the pewter cross half-hanging out of it, the woman has her hand on her mouth like she's eating an apple, and Bela with his hairy Hungarian chest hanging out, is crying "Vilia! Vilia!", which I figured out was the rat's name, and the thing ain't moving. What stood out besides everything else, is hearing him yelling over and over again, "Oh my God!" The cops came, the fire engines came, the EMS wagon came, sirens waking up whoever slept through everything else, lights flashing all over the place--what a night!

And that was the end of Vilia, poor thing! I'm sure the rat-angels carried her to Rat-Heaven, especially since the cops said the cross must have hit the cage and somehow broke the window, batting it down five floors for a home run to the courtyard cement. Now, who do you think the Count blamed for making him swear off his violin sessions with those broads--I mean music students--which he did: Porno Hotalova who corrupted Bela's musical mind with his filthy flicks? At least, that's what I think got him started, but what do I know? Or, maybe the violin babe who I think accidentally grabbed or kicked the crucifix on the wall--don't let me draw pictures of the couch stuff, especially now that Tamara's working on me with her holy habits. Can you guess? You got it! Jesus! He says Jesus did it, and he's not going to believe in God anymore! Screwy! I mean, his logic, you know what I'm saying? What does Jesus have to do with an accident like that? Okay, maybe God punished him. After all, he deserved it, fiddling around like that, but does that mean you turn off Jesus, you turn off God? That's the way it goes! Jesus gets the blame for everybody else's sins 'cause He has none of His own! He took the rap for everybody else. At least that's what those holy rollers say when they meet across the street by the Deli every day unless there's an earthquake, a tornado, or a volcanic eruption! You know, an "Act of God"? How about saying you're sorry and won't do it again, or maybe, you're not sorry and you are going to do it again, and God does not want that poor innocent rat with the pink eyes seeing that kind of stuff, anymore? Vilia, that's her, I could easily forget that name except for Bela's calling out "Oh my God!" You know, I don't think she got pink eyeballs from crying or eyestrain from watching his duets, but she must have found it hard to sleep being right there on the end table. So, no more Ave Maria, no more The Lord's Prayer, remember the "Our Father"?--beautiful stuff, especially the way he played it! You know, he really screwed himself, but he blamed the crucifix, just like Dracula-- thud! A stake in the heart and that was it. Bela Maritza was changed into Bela the Atheist solid Jackson, as they used to say--never heard that one before did you? Now, Bela the Hungarian Atheist and Violinist was even more an atheist than ever before!

Ha! I remember wondering before I went to bed that night, if the ASPCA had any laws against pets seeing whatever he and his student were doing. I let it go because of realizing the animals might like it and there's no way of proving otherwise, although these days who knows what a good rat-psychologist could come up with. They spend a lot of time experimenting with them. Maybe some of them should get arrested for what they do to those poor little things. Maybe alot of women and elephants who get spooked by those little creatures wouldn't agree with me, but then again, not everybody has rat-compassion like me.

Anyway, he moved after that pretty quick, I'd say. No more great violin music, just Porno Hotalova with the loud sound effects and jazzy music from whatever filth he was watching. Too bad, 'cause neighbees shouldn't be that way. We should all stick together like clumps of wet and dry leaves stuck together on the drainholes of the sewer grate at the end of the curb gutter in the street, but I think old Bela stuck together the wrong way and went down the sewer. Too bad. Neighbees are not out for themselves like I think he was. They do Love, Courtesy, and Respect. Even the NYPD at least does Professionalism, Courtesy, and Respect, but not in that order. Look how they came, and quick, too!

I think they really felt it for poor little Vilia, rat that she was! Look at that! Even the cops and the firemen cared more for the rat than he did. I could be wrong about that. What do I know about rat-love, particularly Violinic rat-love? Like that word? I just made it up because "Bela, the lustful atheistic non-atheist" could fiddle quite a bit even without a violin sitting on his shoulder. Some neighbee!

Oh, and just one more thing: those "Acts of God". Maybe there wouldn't be so many of them, if we all got our acts together. Who knows? All I can figure out is the more these Holy Rollers by the Deli make the scene, the more I think they teach me things that I'm not sure they even know about, but because they say them, it affects me in a good way. And they make me feel more guilty about what I feel guilty about. I guess they're the kind of neighbees that sting you for your own good. I could picture Bela standing in the midst of them playing holy music, and the Deli owner becoming so moved that he sent his daughter out there to give him a free Goulash hero. Wait, it would be better if Bela played blindfolded so he wouldn't see the daughter. Why should we light another flame under that Fiddler? She's liable to melt his gold teeth. I can see that, and I'm not one to fiddle around.

CHAPTER ELEVEN

The Bulgarian Bulge

Until you've met "Boring Boris" Dimitrov, you would have no concept of what a mirror-magnet is. This guy is a special kind of neighbee. I only know one but that's all you need to, to know what they look like. Mirrors are never alone, because they'll always draw attention to themselves.

Some decades ago, a hit song was called "The Mirror Song" (by me)--so catchy, so good. It wasn't called that, pretended to be a love song, but you couldn't fool me, I knew it was really "The Mirror Song". Went something like this: "You are too good to be true, can't take my eyes off of you..." Sung I think by Frankie Valli and a bunch of others, and you can be sure none of them knew it was "The Mirror Song". How do I know? Because it was true. Just ask me. And that was the theme song of the Class A mirror-magnet, Boring Boris, a perfect example of one.

Oh, didn't you know there are different classes of them? Well, this chapter is about "The Bulgarian Bulge", and I think you'll have to wait for another book, maybe by me to learn what classes B,C,D,E, and F mirror-magnets look like--who else would know about them?

Boris Dimitrov or "The Bulgarian Bulge" as me, Drinkie, Fulmuna, and Isabella call him, should have owned stocks in the mirror business. Why? His 3rd floor apartment is all mirror-glass. The guy can never be alone. Ever hear that expression, "What am I supposed to do, stay home and look at the four walls?" Well, in his place he never sees four walls, but bulges all over the pad. These are muscles on top of muscles, and they belong to him and are on one, two, four, fourteen, forty reflections of him in those mirrors. Wherever he walks in the place, all that anybody can see is him. Bulging Boris Dimitrov wherever he looks. Who can ever be lonely with so many of themselves looking at them?

Now, that's another thing that gets me going. Am I coming through so far? Do you get the feeling we're mentally clumping here like wet and dry leaves stuck on the drainholes of the steel sewer grate at the end of the curb gutter in the street? I think so.

I hate ceiling mirrors! No, not because they're too far away to see up close without a ladder. It's fear, and I don't think I'm getting hysterical here. It's fear of the unknown. This is Mirror-man staring down at you from the ceiling. he wants to be with you, close to you, even if it means crashing down on your head as you sleep. Hey, get real! You have to be crazy to put mirrors on the ceiling, especially in an apartment complex! Who lives over you? Five hundred and fifty pound Amelia, who does trampoline therapy on her Eclipse mattress with the ever-resilient (hey, that's what the ad said, I think, and Amelia used to be 700, so let's cut her some slack) box spring? Be careful, Cliff Doombrowski, some beds you just don't hide under.

Okay, Amelia doesn't live there, but what if she visits and they have that wild party again on Saturday night, and she goes to get her coat off the bed at 2 a.m., trips over one of the guests sleeping it off on the bedroom floor? Goodbye, guests, goodbye floor, goodbye ceiling of Boring Boris sleeping in bed on the third floor. and maybe goodbye Boris.

No, the life of a mirror-magnet is not for me. But for Boris, it suits him to a "T". He's about fifty, balding, with a big bushy mustache, and muscles on top of his muscles as I said, but since you last read that, there must be more muscles popping up. Must have a set of weights or is a gym freak and did give Isabella a business card saying he is a licensed masseur. Now, get this: Isabella is not flirty, but she does have the neighbee kind of familiarity which could make a guy feel more at home with her than he should--if you catch my verbal vibe. Am I getting to your top floor? Good. She asks the Bulgarian Bulge if he does house calls or has his own parlor. And I'm right there, trying not to laugh, because I see where the "Bulge-o" is going with this--but I could be wrong, also. He tells her with his fat accent--which I like to imitate, it does something for me--that his parlor is in his bedroom, but could be in his living room. So, I'm dying but holding it in, and didn't see this one coming. He comes right out and says "I like to massage people wherever there are mirrors, so they can look, I can look, I want to see them, and more of them, I want to see me, and I want to see them seeing me, and I want to see me seeing them seeing me." After hearing that, I wouldn't have allowed him to massage my pet cockroach. No, let me think about that. Anyway, he continued, "If you can afford sixty dollars an hour with two five minute breaks, I'll be seeing you in all the old familiar places, and you'll be seeing me." Something about that last bit he said made me think he learned English listening to old popular love songs. Oh yeah, I remember his adding, "And also, cash only and in advance." He said all that in one breath, and his bulging chest expanding as he took in another.

So, Isabella asks him if he does men also, and he says "Of course! Moneys is moneys, or as we say in Bulgaria, 'Stotinki is Stotinki, unless you have enough to make a Lev'. This is why I like your name, Stinkie, it reminds me of Stotinki and I feel good, you know, the old contry." (That's the way he says it--who needs "u"?--sorry, no offense meant. And by the way, "Stotinki" and "Lev" are Bulgarian "moneys") His eyes suddenly got that far-away look in them, so I didn't try to remind him I'm Stinko, not Stinkie. Let him have his dream of the good old days, if they were that. If not, why should I be the one to make a stink about it?

Then she asks him if anybody can watch, and he tells her "No problem as long as client doses not object." She asks another, if he'd massage anybody, which I thought was an interesting question. The answer floored me: "Flash is flash, we all have it, but if it is sick flash or dirty flash, I no touch!" "Okay, be picky", I thought. Then I hear it: he won't do if they have different colored eyes! Wow! Suddenly, I'm thinking about Drinkie with the sky-blue right one with raised eyebrow and the greenish-brown left, her "winking" eye for policemen, firemen, and on the postman with shorts and nice knees--Drinkie's words, not mine. Then I'm thinking about Carmelo, the superstitious owner-of-nice-knees postman. Don't ask, I'll tell you why in a sec, you see, Drinkie's good stuff, a real neighbee! She says now and then, as you know, "Stinko, you are the man, and I'm the woman, and they be our neighbees all around us." And there we are, fast friends like clumps of wet and dry leaves stuck together on the drainholes of the steel sewer grate at the end of the curb gutter in the street.

Now, Carmelo seems like a nice guy, but I don't think he's too bright. Oh, he's good with the postal stuff, I'm sure, but catch this: I notice each time Drinkie winks at him, he nods with a tiny smile, I think, but then crosses himself and mumbles in some Spanish, and he never stops to talk but I see him talking with others like Boring Boris, the Bulging Bulgarian. How about that? So, I ask Bulge-O why no massage for the rainbow-eyed like Drinkie, and he says it brings bad evil if you touch someone who has them, and I tell him that's probably an old Bulgarian superstition. He says even her uncle says so. Her uncle? Then I'm thinking about Grandpa Bert. When I mentioned him, the Bulge says, "No, the fat man she lives with." He's talking about Fulmuna! Aha! It all clicks. Fulmuna told the Bulge he's Drinkie's uncle and for his own good he doesn't touch her. Then either Bulge-O or Fulmuna got to Carmelo. For Fulmuna, I could see it because he's seen her winking at the knee-man and is a little sick in the brain from his peep-o-rama midnight roof arrangements--if you catch my swift chickenhawk of a thought.

For the Bulge, either he and kneeman are sharing their favorite fears or they both have the same superstition, and Boring Boris is pushing his this-month-only sensational massage offer, his famous 3-hand massage. Don't ask me how he does it, maybe with a rubber glove on one foot, but what about all those mirrors? Somebody's got to see him do it.

I can't think about all this jazz. All I know is Fulmuna is protecting his marriage so he thinks, by being a good uncle, and keeping the sausage fingers of the Bulgarian Bulge off his wife's back. Pretty good, yes? And one last thing about how the Fulmuna covers his story with Carmelo: he probably tells him the "Mr. and Mrs." on the envelopes of his mail is because he is a widower and Drinkie is his late nephew's wife who took him in out of pity.

I don't have to ask Drinkie about all this. If Bulge-o asks about it, I'll tell him I like Drinkie but don't trust her or her Uncle or Husband or whatever they are together, and that talking about them could bring bad luck, and that will be that. Muscles are no match for a spooky superstition, not even nice knees, if you catch my firefly brainwaves.

Do you follow all this stuff? It can make you nuts. But not me, I'm there already and managing it pretty good, wouldn't you say? Forget it—don't answer.

Another thing: I notice Boring Boris seeming to invest confidence in me. First I thought it was just body language, but then he reinforces it by asking me a winner: "Mr. Stinkie, do you think I am a peeping john?" I asked him, "Who told you that, Boris? And by the way, it is 'Peeping tom', not 'john'." "Oh yes, that's him!" he said and nodded, then seemed to lift up his massive frame to a Marine posture, and explained, "Uncle Fulmunie told me that I live in a house of mirrors and everytime I see me or anyone else in them, I'm as good as a spy and bad things can come from that."

Good thing I wasn't eating at that moment. I know I would have choked for sure. Look at that! Fulmuna on a roof under the full moon.

Him and Boobie deal, and now he's putting the double whammy--I think that's how you say it—on this bulging bicep guy who can bulge everything except his Bulgarian brain.

I wish I could end this chapter saying this is neighbees courtesy, love, and respect not as the NYPD who does Professionalism instead of love because that's the job, and when they do, love in the Professionalism. It doesn't always make the Press or the broadcasters, because we know bad news is what sells, not good news--we know the game--we know it good, if you catch my law and order secret message. Give the cops a break, they have a target painted on the back of their uniform. If you back them up more often instead of the creeps, maybe we'd have more roaches on the run instead of them doing their thing right in front of us. Wow, where did that come from? Oh yeah, we were wishing we could end the chapter one way, but instead I have to end it saying neighbees are real slick and screwy at times, and make me wonder how these things work to help them clump together like wet and dry leaves, stuck on the drainholes of the steel sewer grate at the end of the curb gutter in the street. Ever feel like you've said something before, and you have?

CHAPTER TWELVE

The Iceman Cometh & Goeth

Now look, I've got a few more clumpies to give you so you'll know all the important things about how neighbees should be. And then, for a grand finale, I'll give you an unbelievable surprise report on Tamara Yestadey, which should make you say "Holy God!" or which a devout Jew might say, "Holy G-d!", although it's very hard to say it without the "o", and maybe it would be better if such a person would say "Holy G-d!, a three letter word for the Almighty, starting with 'G', ending with 'd', and a dash in between for which missing vowel? You have twenty seconds to answer or you'll be in eternal jeopardy!" And then hum the Jeopardy tune and tap your foot. This is a bit much, as I'm sure you agree, so how about just "Holy G!"

Before that finale, I've got to tell you about Drinkie's Grandpa. He's ninety-three and lives in the basement here--yeah, there are two three-room apartments there. That's one story, and the second is about Santo Giancomezzi, who lived there before him. This proves beyond the shadow of a doubt that a six-story building can have two stories in the basement.

Let me tell you about Santo first. There were two apartments in the basement, one was for a Super, you know, a Superintendent who takes care of the whole building, and the other was for a handyman who assisted him. Drinkie's Grandpa was the Super, qualified because he knew plumbing, heating, and even electrical stuff. Santo was the handyman. Now, this building is old, and at one time there was a dumbwaiter. Do you know what I'm talking about? This was not a stupid person who worked in a restaurant, but a small garbage elevator that went up and down a shaft so each apartment dweller could dispose of their garbage without carrying it down to some pails. A door in each apartment was opened by the tenant after the handyman in the basement rope-hoisted the little elevator compartment, a four foot tall by a foot and a half deep and wide, to their dumbwaiter door and rang a buzzer. It was usually about seven in the p.m. when everybody was home, sometimes eating dinner, which was not a welcome time for such service.

Anyway, they put their trash in it, and there were no such things as plastic bags back then, so it was paper bags, leaky, rippy, drippy, smelly bags smelling as bad as the shaft. The hoisting rope was like the ones used to tie boats to a dock. And you can imagine how the handyman had to labor as if he were Quasimodo, the Hunchback of Notre Dame, ringing the bell, but instead he was Trashimodo, and the easy part was ringing the buzzer. The only hunch he had was that people were willing to get rid of their garbage even though he was interrupting their dinner, that is, if he was on time.

So you can figure I'm talking about the 1940's before I was even born. The author is older than me, so he probably knows about dumbwaiters. Now, if people missed the buzzing, like say you were on the bowl, you get the picture? Tough! You had to either wait 'til the next night--meaning partytime to the roaches, or bring the bags all the way down to the basement yourself.

Also, the Handyman's job was to take turns with the Super, shoveling coal into the furnace to make heat and hot water. And more, they had to remove the ashes from the furnace, put them in heavy steel-banded steel barrels, which then were put on the side of the building for the garbage truck to pick up. This was before oil was used in the boiler to heat it and make steam. What a relief it must have been when they converted from coal to oil! No more shoveling, hauling ash cans--that's what garbage cans were called then--get it? And that coal was delivered by coal trucks that would pour it from the truck by a steel chute through a basement window into the cellar, which had a walled-in pen there called the "coal bin".

What a process! Some trucks offloaded the coal into big wooden barrels, then rolled them over to the chute-window and upended them. Oof! Such heavy labor!

At some point back then the landlord stopped using the dumbwaiter system, and tenants had to bring the garbage down to the basement. That meant the handyman had a lot less to do. His pay was free rent and whatever tips people threw him for the dumbwaiter service. So, clever guy that he was, he made a deal to stay in the apartment, give the landlord thirty bucks a month rent--it was only two rooms--put out the garbage pails--no longer ash cans by then, and shovel snow in the winter. Oh yes, and sweep around once a week, mopping the tiled floor halls with "CN", nice-smelling cleaning stuff Grandpa Bert says he liked.

Everybody was happy, including Mrs. Rafkind, a retired schoolteacher who couldn't stand the dumbwaiter service because she liked to read on the bowl, don't ask how anybody knew that, but that's what happens when neighbees live in the same building, everybody gets to know your business; so, Raffy almost always missed the erratic dumbwaiter buzzer which sometimes could be off by almost an hour! That's a long time on the bowl, but then again, as a schoolteacher, maybe she was marking homework papers there—ugh! She'd also make a big stink about the stench that came from the dumbwaiter shaft, because of all the drooly stuff that soaked the lift, I guess, and maybe some gooey stuff or worse that fell off it through the dissolving paper bags. Conk! I'm not sure the dumbwaiter guy wore a helmet all the time, but the last one, Santo, owned a World War One German helmet with a spike on top, I guess to impale rotten grapefruits or something.

Madame Rafkind also wrote letters to the Health department about roaches and rats, not rats like Vilia, poor Vilia--not so little. Remember? Count Maritza? Some violinist! The Concertmaster Whoremaster, or maybe I shouldn't use such language? I agree. Let me take it back and instead call him a "Whoremaestro", sounds more dignified, yes? Anyway, Mrs. Rafkind, or "Lady Bookworm" as they called her around here, got a reply from the Health department that the Landlord told them they had evidence she was throwing her garbage bags down the shaft and was responsible for the infestation if there was one: herself!

Further, the Landlord sent her a separate letter saying they took fingerprints off the jar of pickled herring and creamed whitefish often found in those bags--yuck! Excuse me, I shouldn't knock anybody else's delights just because they may be on my "Food-hate" list with yogurt at the top, but let's face it, some things are beyond comprehension, even if you try to cover for it by saying "Oh, but you have to try it with fruit in it!" No I don't! Yogurt is yogurt, and maybe now if I call it "Yuckgurt", they'll get the message not to try and fruitify for me! Now, what happened to old lady Rafkind?

Oh yeah, the Landlord's son was a Criminal Investigator, and when he let her know that in his letter, she dropped the issue and no more jars or cans down the shaft. I don't think she's still living. Anyway, she dropped the issue and no more garbage bags kissed the Dumbwaiter head while it rested on the shaft floor, and she is probably still sitting on a bowl somewhere in Heaven or Hell, maybe with Trashimodo buzzing her day and night--sounds to me like Hell. Never was much of a neighbee, the way I hear.

How do I know all these things? Drinkie's Grandpa! The man is a walking history book! By the way, his name is Umberto Dellacroce, or "Grandpa Bert" as Drinkie calls him.

So that's how it was in this place, a real classy apartment house, wouldn't you say?

Okay, let's first cover Santo Giancomezzi, or "Sonny", as I said I would. Ha! Sonny! And he lived in the basement where there never was any sun unless you walked into the alleyway twice a day, once around 10 a.m. and then about 3 p.m depending on the season, and if there were no clouds. I know, I know, "Sonny" is not the same as "Sunny". You're telling me? Wait 'til you hear what this "dark star" does!

I think about 1948, Sonny starts to pay thirty a month rent to keep the apartment. He then gets a part-time job in the Ice, Kerosene, and Coal business, another dying enterprise when the oil burners replaced coal furnaces, and refrigerators replaced ice boxes, and the automatic feed of oil into the burner meant that tenants didn't need to freeze their padded parts off waiting for coal to be shoveled into the furnace. That was the kiss of death for the kerosene stove, which didn't have a great track record for safety and people who loved their lungs--God knows what else.

So, Sonny's got a wife, Lena, maybe Common Law, who's always walking around in pajamas and a housecoat--very revealing, draw your own picture. But she's not pushing anything according to Grandpa Bert, just a friendly pajama girl with buck teeth, and if Judy Garland had been ugly, that's what she looked like--these are Grandpa Bert's words, not mine, because I kind of like buck teeth on women, don't ask why, I do not know. And she's not singing "Somewhere Over The Rainbow". She goes around that apartment and the alleyway singing, "I've got the sun in the morning and the moon at night". This was a song Judy Garland sang around then, and Grandpa Bert hears her singing "Got no diamonds, got no pearl, still I think I'm a lucky girl..." and also "Got no mansion, got no yacht, but still I'm happy with what I've got...". And what does she "got"? She's got the sun in the morning and the afternoon sometimes, and a crumb of a husband named Sonny, the Ice Man, who was not nice to kids, always chasing them out of the alleyway and the cellar--sort of can't blame him, because he lived down there with windows in the alleyway where the kids liked to play punchball. But Grandpa Bert said he made the newspapers and went to jail for a few years, and his singing wife took off while he was doing time, probably having found sun in the morning and the moon at night somewhere else where it was safer.

Here's why: Grandpa Bert said Sonny on his Ice, Coal, and Kerosene route started doing things with Italian immigrant wives--you know, "War Brides"? And somehow he convinced them somebody had put an "evil eye" on them, called "Mal Occhio", and only by paying him five bucks a month plus some secret sex, could the spell be broken. They had to wear a chain around their neck with a small padlock on it, and when he came to collect on his ice route, he'd remove the padlock with his key, then give them a "treatment"--don't make me draw pictures. He somehow convinced them that anytime they got sick, it was "Mal Occhio", and they should call him instead of the doctor.

How'd he get caught? I thought you'd never ask. One of his "patients", that is, victims, had a neighbee who had migraines, so, the victim says it may be an evil spirit, and gets "Dr. Sonny" on the case, who then makes a house call, as doctors used to do all the time back then, and her husband, a Police Captain, came home unexpectedly while she was being "treated", so Dr. Sonny got a worse headache physically, and then somehow everything came out and the Brooklyn Eagle or the Journal American, which Grandpa Bert says were newspapers at that time, ran a few articles on Sonny the Ice Man who was not Sonny the nice man.

And his poor but happy wife, Lena? Grandpa Bert doesn't know where she went, but because of the way she sang, he said with a smile, he was sure it was somewhere over the rainbow with the sun in the morning and the moon at night. I think I already told you that, but it amuses me to repeat what he said. Grandpa gave me the impression that the guy never fit in like clumps of wet and dry leaves stuck together on the drainholes of the sewer grate at the end of the curb gutter in the street, but was definitely sewer material. I added in my "clumps" parable because Grandpa Bert had other words for Dr. Sonny, more sewer-like.

Okay, he's done, down the drain as far as neighbees go, and you'll have to wait for the next chapter to hear some stuff about Grandpa Bert, the super-Super. "Hang in there!" is now one of my favorite ways of saying "Stay tuned!", if you can absorb my lynch language. I keep learning here, even after all these years. You know, an informed, educated neighbee can make it easier on everybody including the NYPD who loves to do Courtesy, Professionalism, and Respect. The Ice man is gone, along with the Dumbwaiter, the Coal truck and the ash cans, but the NYPD is still with us, and they consider your neighbees worth the Courtesy, Love, and Respect, is that CLeaR? You gotta be wondering if the author of this stuff I'm telling you is getting something on the side from the department or maybe the city, right? Well, forget it, it ain't so, and if you don't believe that, ask me.

CHAPTER THIRTEEN

Umberto Loves Alba Madonna In The Bathtub

Now let me tell you about Grandpa Umberto Dellacroce. He had a six room apartment in the basement for decades since "Dr." Santo Giancomezzi got busted for "malpractice". First he paid thirty bucks a month for the extra three rooms, which originally were two but he made three out of them!

Then he worked out a deal to get both places for four hundred a month. We're talking about a six-room flat now--as he calls it. The guy is amazing! He still shovels a little snow, but mainly uses a snowblower. The new Super, Carlos, has a four-roomer on the first floor, and he depends a lot on Grandpa Bert for knowhow and a lot of things because of the experience. Now get this: If this doesn't blow you away, nothing will! Are we connecting? Say "Yes!" so I can go on. The Landlord's name is Ephraim Berg--he's loaded and inherited the property from his Grandfather Shlomo Berg. His wife Magdalena is a big woman, I mean "Big!" And Bergie is tiny by comparison. She hugs him swallowing him in her arms! You gotta look for him somewhere buried in the midst of her pillowy pontoons. He'll never drown in deep water with her! They love opera and she can sing like one of those big women, I think the German ones that have a helmet and blonde pigtails, with horns sticking out of the helmet. What a voice comes out of that chest! Bergie loves her cooking. He gave up Leo's Kosher Deli for her cooking! And Leo's is top-drawer eating! But even her meatball/ matzoh ball combination soup leaves Leo in the dust.

Oh yeah, and by the way, I think I was too young to remember this, but Grandpa Bert says that back in his days if you went into a meat store, there was sawdust all over the floor! I guess it was left over from the batch they added to the chopmeat--just kidding--don't get nervous. But that's what he said they had. Imagine the women with open-toed shoes, getting splinters in their big toe--ouch! He also said if you dropped your change, you might have a problem finding it in that sea. Maybe that's where they got that saying, "Leave it for the sweeper!" You never can tell. Another gem about big Magdalena is that she also made a chopped liver and onion dip with mushrooms that would knock your tonsils off! Maybe that's why Grandpa Bert got tonsillitis every winter according to Drinkie.

Now, twenty-five years ago before Grandpa Bert retired, she's going down the basement with "Fry-Me", which is Berg's nickname and spelled "Phraimey", to see Grandpa about something. Isn't that wild? Tamara's maiden name is "Sleighme", and they both rhyme! Amazing stuff. Imagine if "rhyme" were pronounced "rhy-me"! What a kick in the head! But who wants to be kicked there?

Anyway, back to the basement where the action is, or was. So, Mrs. Berg, Magdalena or "Maggie" for short, stops Bergie on the steps down to the "dungeon", as she used to call it--according to Drinkie, and asks, "Phraimey, what's that smell?" So, he says "Garbage, what else?" "No, no," she says, "I know that smell! That's Alba Madonna!" So, Bergie thinks she's cursing, but she says, "No, 'Alba Madonna' is Italian for 'White truffle', you know, the mushrooms I use to make your favorite Tomato and Mushroom salad?" "So, somebody threw out garbage with mushrooms in it!" he says, and she starts yelling and cursing, "Phraimey, you_____!" I can't repeat what she called him, but meanwhile, Grandpa Bert, who's in the tool room, comes out and says hello and asks them what's going on. He said she looked like she was going to kill him with a flaming eyes maneuver, as if she was wearing the helmet with the horns in a German opera, you know, the look that could kill? Talk about "Mal Occhio"! This was a double whammy with those boobie eyes popping out of her head--no reference here to Slutta, who didn't live here then. Bergie says "Umberto, help! Sing an aria to calm this woman down!"

So, Grandpa says, "I confess! I heard her yelling 'Alba Madonna', and I knew the jig was up! I can't hide it any longer. I hope you won't get mad at me! I hate to get rid of them." So, Bergie says, "What the hell are you talking about? She's ready to kill me and you're confessing to what? Is there a connection here?" With that, Grandpa takes them to the old coal bins where the coal chute used to dump the coals through the cellar window before the oil burner conversion. There, he's got eight old style porcelain tubs, you know, the ones with the four lion's paws holding it up? They're filled with dirt and some strange-looking thin trees and shrubs on top, and a lot of green and brown mold, and he's got some fluorescent plant lights hanging over them like the ones over the pool tables at the P.D.Cue Lounge near the train yards.

Now, I learned a little about mushrooms about which I know nothing and really don't want to know anything, and as a good neighbee I can't hog it to myself--hang in there, I'll also tell you a little about hogs. You see, "Truffle" is the name for the "fruiting" part of an underground mushroom, and also for a very gifted hog.

The Alba Madonna is the name for a special white truffle that grows in the Piedmont section of Northern Italy, and right there in the country area around the city of Alba. See the name connection? Good.

So, I learned there are two animals used by mushroom growers in Europe, particularly Italy and France. One is the Truffle hog, the other the Truffle hound. These four-legged miracle smelling machines can sniff out Alba Madonnas like you can't figure! If you use the Truffle hog, you gotta be fast, because he'll eat it as soon as he finds it, so that name "hog" is no accident when it comes to food. The Truffle hound has far more manners. But, there you go, and Maggie, the mushroom-hunter could be something beyond human, like part Truffle hog and Truffle dog, or "hound" sounds better, rhyming with "ground".

Can you imagine? She smells something under the ground! Maybe that's where she dug up little Bergie! No, forget that last crack; Bergie's really a nice man, just keep him eating those Tomato and Mushroom salads. Now, back to the basement.

Bergie is stunned, if you connect with the scene--know what I'm saying? He goes, "What is this? I thought you had tools here!" "No." Grandpa tells him, "I keep them in the apartment and these lights are powered by the electric extension from my kitchen, if you follow this overhead conduit pipe." With that, Maggie shifts from rage to rejoicing at the same decibel level. She's panting like she's treading water, if you can size up my prose here; her chest starts expanding, then sinking a bit, and she just about stutters, "Um, ah Umberto, you grow Alba's here?" That was it! You could say he signed a lifetime lease down there! They haven't raised his rent since, and at ninety three now, he's become her source--which means their source--for White truffles.

Drinkie says she thinks the Bergs have some kind of deal going with him, aside from just supplying Alba Madonnas for her sauce, soups, and Tomato Mushroom salad. Now, what is that about? Forget I said it-- don't quote me. I think the Fulmuna/Boobie Bathing Beauty contest has affected her mind. Doesn't matter, she's still the woman, Fulmuna is the husband, I'm the man, and they be our neighbees all around us, I think.

Wild stuff, hah? I'm talking mushrooms. I wouldn't even eat a grocery store one--I don't trust any of those things--wouldn't even eat a green potato, know what I'm saying? Anyway, Grandpa Bert is here for life and he looks like he's gonna outlive the Bergs, but then again, maybe those Albas are going to keep the three of them alive to one hundred and thirty! You never can tell! Imagine all three of them croaking at once when a poison mushroom sneaks into the bathtub and does them in? I could picture Grandpa laid out in one of those bathtubs--have the wake right there in the cellar! No casket--save money--Drinkie gets everything anyway. Whatever he's got. Then, for the funeral, just cover him with Alba Madonna dirt, and bingo! He'll be there for Eternity, pushing up the mushrooms—who needs daisies? I know I get carried away, but why should he? Just send the embalmer downstairs and finito! Done! As he always says after knocking off another plumbing challenge, "Santa Madonna!" I think it's because of his knees when he has to crouch.

Okay! That's what I had to say about Umberto Dellacroce. By the way, you probably didn't notice, but I don't say things anymore like "You know what I mean?" so often, you get what I'm saying? And also, did you notice I didn't mention in this chapter anything about the NYPD who does--by now you should have it memorized. Here's a hint: C_____P_____R_____. You fill in the blanks.

CHAPTER FOURTEEN

Holy Hotski

Now, this should slay you just like it would slay me if I was where you are, that is, if you're still there. Hello? Okay, just checking. I gotta tell you about Yestadey, that is, today, about Tamara Yestadey and Hotalova who was Hotalova Yestadey, but today? Well, you're not gonna believe this, but what else is new? Who the fruitcake believes anything today? I could have said "Who the hell", or other things, but instead I made it a fruitcake, feeling better saying that because I don't like hell and come to think of it, I don't like fruitcake either! Do you? Does anybody? This has been a gripe with me for many years. If not, then why do they buy that crap? Oops, strike that from the record, as a judge would say. I'll try to say "parc"--that's "crap" backwards--instead, doing the backward shift, and let's leave the "f" in the shift to show a difference between me and dirty Boobie--what a piece of, uh, work he is! See, I almost slipped, but don't worry, I'll get it right before this book is done.

Oh yeah, you're not gonna believe what happened here the day after dirty Boobie broke our motto, you know, "Love, Courtesy, and Respect" and so on, etc., etc.? Get this: Tamara and me are having breakfast on the stoop--weather's real nice, and she made some French toast sandwiches with Canadian bacon, my favorite. And who gets out of a cab sharp as a Salami hero sandwich with a dozen slices of extra-aged cheddar cheese, if you catch the soap bubbles I'm blowing your way. Isn't that better than "Get the picture?"? You got it. The big man, the "Hotski"! It's him, Hotalova! I almost choked on the Canadian bacon, and would have had to be helicoptered to Montreal for surgery! He looked like a trillion bucks! That's right, we're past talking about millions or even billions. This is the Twenty-first century, and bingo! What's new? It's him, a new man! He's got a big gold-edged Bible, and a smile I never saw on him before. "Praise the Lord, Tamara!" he spouts, like a football coach egging on his team at half-time, then turns to me: "The Lord Bless you, Stinko! Isn't it a great day Jesus is giving us?"

Tamara is ogling him with big meatball eyes popping. These are not flaming boobie eyes like Maggie Berg's, and it's not Mal Occhio's like what Sonny the Ice Man could cure with a padlock for cash and sex "treatments", this was big, holy meatball eyes! First, I got concerned that she's dropping dead right in front of us with her eyes open, then I see, she's rearranging the French toast in her mouth so the Montreal helicopter won't be needed. Then, he stoops over because we're sitting on the stoop, and embraces her like as if to make the meatballs pop out over his shoulder and roll down the walk, and I'm stunned, but thinking this is how neighbees should be, like clumps of wet and dry leaves stuck together on the drainholes of the steel sewer grate at the end of the curb gutter in the street, even if the meatballs roll off the sidewalk into the gutter and get there first. And she pushes him away, stands up, pulling on her long skirt which was sticking to her, swallows the French Canadian mouthful, and opens her mouth to speak, with the weirdest look and half-squint on her face.

"Honey," he says, "Don't say a word and don't offer me a French toast Canadian bacon sandwich, I'm fasting today. And, by the way, I'm saved! I gave my heart to Jesus and now the only porno book I read is the Bible, but it's not 'Porno-again!' I'm 'Born-again'! Hallelujah, and Glory to His Holy Name!"

So, Tamara is sort of like shaking her head--sort of reassembling the nuts and bolts of her brain. Then, she says, "Hotsky, maybe you're trying out for a part in a play or movie. Let me know where and when it opens or is in the theater, I'll come and see it. You're doing this very good! I guess we should now talk about divorce. Why else are you here?" "Divorce?" he asks, "No, unless that's what you need to do--it looks like you two are into--what was that, Stinko? Something about, um, love, honor, and uh, what the NYPD does. Oh yes, professionality--wasn't that it?" "You're close, Hotalova," I said, "I do have love and respect and courtesy with your Missus!" And Tamara whips in: "His Missus? I'm nobody's Missus, Stinko!" "Okay, okay, sorry Tamara," I said, and addressing him again with "What I mean is, I'm Tamara's friend the same way I am with Drinkie, just want to be a good neighbee, but I wouldn't close the door on something serious happening, and if it did, it has to be love, respect, and courtesy--I don't believe in complicating my life or any woman's with sex issues. To me, neighbees are family, so that kind of crap is out (I remember that I forgot to say it backwards, you know, "parc", like I said I would?). I can tell you Tamara's the same as she was when you left; a good decent woman, a real holy broad, if you get the picture."

"Please, Stinko, don't give the Hotski the impression I've been saving myself for him!", Tamara spouts, "I've had two years of purity in this place and I'm no 'Broad'! As far as I'm concerned it's going to stay that way as long as I can afford the rent, no thanks to anyone else!" Then, Hotalova makes his case: "No, Tam, I just want to apologize and talk things over with you." That was my cue. "Sorry folks, how about I'll leave you two?" "No, no, Stinko," she protests, "stay right here, I may need a witness. This is unbelievable, and I'm sure not going to fall for it!" Then, the Hotski puts out his hands, palms up like he's going to make a speech, and says, "Okay, then I'll give you both my testimony if you will hear it." "Testimony?" she pops off, kind of loud, "What are you, in a court case? Huh! Probably with Larry Flynt or Hugh Hefner, I guess! I think one of them is also 'saved', but I heard somewhere the magazine is still in business, whichever one it was. The subscriptions stopped a short time after you left. Probably on-forwarded to your new sleaze-pad!"

She was starting to steam. Then the Hotski shrugs, "I don't know, Tam. I'd like to date you even though we're married." And she slams him with " 'Estranged' is more like it, Mister!" Oof! I could feel the iceberg closing in on the stoop, but he brushed it aside! "In spite of that and me, Tam, how about going to church with me tonight after I take you to dinner?" "Dinner? Church! Pinch me somebody, this is unreal!" she says, again with the meatball eyes, a little moist I could tell. I felt it in the throat for her. So, I asked, "Hotski, what kind of church is it? Do you go there, like often?" "Oh yes, Stinko," he tells me, "I've been going there for the last seven months, four times a week." With that Tamara jumps in the ring to pummel him again: "You? Four times a week? And what kind of DVD's are they playing there?" "I know, Tam," he replies, looking down and shaking his head like in agreement, "I can't believe it myself. You'd have to come and see." "See what? I've got my own church!" she shoots back. "Okay," he says, putting his head down, but smiling like I never saw him before, even when he showed me a centerfold that burned his fingers--what a difference! "Then let's just do dinner, and I'll leave you earlier!" he offers. "No, no,

Hot, I'm curious about this and your church. Let's do both. So, what are you doing here besides the date invitation?" she asks. And he says, "I've got a lot of apologizing to do." "Oh!" she pops out, like someone poked her. That was my cue to take off, so I said, "Tamara, thanks so much for the sandwich--delicious, as always. I've gotta take care of things now." Then I shook his hand, saying "Hotski, I never saw you like this--amazing! I'm gonna go drop dead somewhere!" Wrong words, because then he hits me with, "Not without Jesus, Stinko! We must talk very soon. It's real good stuff!" "Okay, Hotski, we'll do it!" I said, nodding and giving him two thumbs up, and with that I backed into the apartment house lobby, sort of shaky in the legs from the shock--if you can grab that--and a bit feeling good to see a hint of a sparkle in those moist and cute meatball eyes of Tamara.

Wow! Strange stuff! I guess the next thing to expect is a centerfold of Tamara in holy clothes in his church magazine, if they have one. And if you catch my vision, double wow! You know, I have a good feeling about the Yestadeys, like they're gonna get back together again, but better than before, if you're reading my tea leaves. And that's how they should be, not just husband and wife, which sometimes could be like North Korea, South Korea, if you know geography and history--do they teach that anymore? No, they should be like neighbees, you know, like clumps of wet and dry leaves stuck together on the drainholes of the steel sewer grate at the end of the curb gutter in the street. And, if they do that, they will practice Love, Courtesy, and Respect, like the NYPD, except the Bulls do Professionalism instead of Love. Yeah, they have to, like we have to do ours.

CHAPTER FIFTEEN

Who's The Man?

There we are, me and Fulmuna, like, how do they say: two bumps on a log? I think so. But because we're there so regularly, anybody passing by probably says to themselves, "There they are, two bums on the stoop!"

And what that person doesn't know is that we are there to solve the world's problems! Not all together, of course, but with finality, you know, "finito!" as Grandpa Bert says after knocking off another handyman job like some guy one quarter of his age could only hope one day to do-- maybe!

Now, who's doing that today? Not handyman jobs, but solving world problems on a stoop? That's right, nobody! How do I know? It's obvious. They're not sitting here with us.

Look what happened the other night--we dodged a bullet! That's the latest expression. I'm not crazy about it. Sounds too defensive for me. Not a real slug, of course, but—

Oh, wait! Let me just tell you what happened: out of the blue--yeah, it was, because the time was about 11:20 on a clear night. Drinkie went upstairs to make a call to their son, Benny, in Vegas--he works in one of the casinos--I forgot which.

Anyway, Fulmuna says "Stinko, I gotta ask you about something that's been bugging me all week. If Drinkie comes down, we cut it, got it?" "I gotcha, Ful, what's the bug?" I asked. He shakes his head and makes a face: "It's Drinkie. I've gotta put you on the machine." "Machine? What machine?" I came back with, thinking maybe his roof-arrangement with the Boob is affecting his mind. Those kind of lust-things have a way of twisting your brain, if you catch my creme donuts. "The lie detector, what the hell else?" "Whoa!" I said, "Am I going to trial afterwards or before? When have I ever told you a lie?" "That's what's bugging me, Stink," he says, "far as I know, never!"

Then, turning to me with the Father Rutuolo holy fisheyes look, he asks, "Are you and Drinkie 'CLR' people or what?" Of course I knew where he was going, but still felt stunned, like after getting conked in the bleachers at Yankee Stadium with a home run ball. So, shocked as I was, I hit him between the eyes so to say, with "Fulmuna, let me tell you something. We're way beyond Courtesy, Love, and Respect. With us it's Courtesy, Love, and Reverence! And let me tell you, sometime ago, I hear you snoring like a two hundred fifty pound squirrel on the roof with those spyglasses, remember? And I have to confess, I was tempted to look at Drinkie in her bathing suit, but you sneezed, and I said 'God bless you!' and woke you up. Remember? Well, I called you and the Boob-head 'sick' for what you were doing, and look how easy it was for me to get sick also! Now, I'm not a Catholic, but I have to tell you, that bothered me ever since, so much so that I wanted to confess it to Father Rutuolo so if there's a hell, I wouldn't go there for something like that! But since I'm not Catholic, I've been thinking of talking to Holy Hotski about it, maybe even checking out his church, and you're welcome to join me, if you want. Now, what the 'hell' do you think about that?" I had to calm down, feeling the pressure gauge getting a hernia with that push up on the dial, if you get my calisthenic connection. Fulmuna felt the heat and showed the kind of neighbee he was: "Stinko, listen man, I'm sorry for setting you off, but this is what happened: on two nights I wake up hearing Drinkie talking in her sleep. Tuesday night, that is, 3:30 Wednesday morning, she says in her sleep, 'Stinko, Fulmuna is the husband, but you're the man! I think we have to tell him!' Then, last night, same thing! Stinko, what gives? Do you have something to tell me? What am I supposed to think? Tell me something! For God's sake, what is it?" Wow! He was ready for lift-off! And, the volume level had wings also! I had nothing to tell him, so that's what I told him: "Fulmuna, I have nothing to tell you, but Drinkie is the one who can tell both of us, that is, if she knows what's playing in her pretty head in the wee hours."

"Ahah! See! 'Pretty head'! Of course!" he interrupted. I cut in with "Stop, Ful! She's very pretty, what am I supposed to do, lie about that? Stop killing your guts, let's get to Drinkie right now, both of us. As soon as she gets off the phone with Benny, I'm sure she'll be down again, right? So, let's cool it and wait a bit." No sooner I said that and the Drink comes out with a big smile and spouts, "Hey Grandpa Ful, Teresa's gonna be a mama!" Fulmuna just nods with a closed mouth. "What's wrong, Ful?" she asks, looking from him to me and back, "What's with you guys?"

And so, the rest of the dialogue proved to the Ful and also to the full, that you can't count your ducks before their eggs get laid. No, I think it's chickens, right? This is America. But, same difference, right? Are we clicking here? Not Clucking, clicking!

Drinkie's real good at remembering things and also good at forgetting what should be forgotten. If I needed a wife or maybe should say, wanted a wife, it would be someone like her. But, I'm not wishing anything because the way things are, works just fine with me, I think. By the way, Drinkie tells us Tamara invited her to attend the Hotski's church with her, and to take Fulmuna if he'll go. She didn't mention me, so, when she asked what about me, Tamara said it's up to Drinkie! Well, thank you, Tamara! I could have gotten real stung with that one, but for peace of mind I thought, I'm the man, but he's the husband. Then, Drinkie explains she didn't think Fulmuna would want to go, and she was struggling with the thought of going with me first, but telling the Ful what we were doing.

So, guess what? All is calm, all is bright, round yon Virgin Mother and Child, and Fulmuna the husband makes it a silent night and says, "Stinko, you go. You're the man!" And Drinkie says, "See? That's why I had those dreams! You make me talk in my sleep! What do you have, 'Spyglass guilt'?" Now she's glaring at him with the sky-blue eye and raised eyebrow, and the greenish-brown left one reserved for winking at Policemen, Firemen, and Carmelo, the Postman with the shorts and nice knees--her words, not mine, remember? So then I have to eat my "Silent Night" lyrics and told myself it's time to go, like recently when Tamara started to unload, or so I thought, on the Holy Hotski back from the dead and grateful, yes, bigtime!

Then the Fulmuna cops out like the dedicated peeping tom he is and says, "I'm not ready for religion, Drinkie, you guys go. Stink is the man, you're the woman, I'm the husband, and they be our neighbees all around, and even though I'm copping out--no insult to the real cops, the NYPD who do Courtesy, Professionalism, and Respect, which they have to--" "Stop, Ful!" she breaks in with, "I know the saying! Why don't you just go up to the roof and make love to your spyglasses, and I'll enjoy the stoop with Stinko, and then do my moonbathing for your perverted pleasure!" Fulmuna sees me making a move to go, and uses my shoulder to help lift his massiveness off the steps, and says, "No, Stinko, stay, enjoy the Courtesy, Love, and Reverence you guys graduated to, and I'll do my nightwatch until you can help me graduate also." Drinkie shook her head, and helped him up, too, saying, "I'm sorry Ful, I'll be up shortly." What kind of relationship is that, I wondered. Maybe it is one of the mysteries of marriage I may get to know or maybe will never be able to figure, you know what I'm trying to say, do you get my--Oh wait! I forgot about telling you about the bullet we dodged. What was that about? Ah, it'll come to me, we're not finished yet. Probably had something to do with wet and dry leaves stuck together on the drainholes of the steel sewer grate at the end of the curb gutter in the street. Let me think.

And while I'm thinking about it, I don't see how Drinkie's gonna go to Hotski's church without Fulmuna, and even though he now knows what she was talking about in her sleep, I think I'll just lay low on this and wait for Tamara and the Hotski to practically beg me to go. It gives me some kind of power to see them all eager for me to get involved with their faith houses, and me to decide like I'm some sort of spoiled brat they don't want to upset while I say, "Eenie, meenie, miney, moe; to which house of worship should I go?".

You know, a thought just occurred to me about El Peepo. What if someone else saw him on the roof with his binoculars? Could he get arrested for being a Peeping Tom? And then, if there is such a law, what if he told them it's his wife-o? I wouldn't put it past Fulmuna to peep out his wife, saying to the NYPD Officers they can join him anytime, when off duty, of course. I mean if him and Boobie can do these things, what's to stop him from corrupting the Bulls? I mean, Cops.

Have to stop calling them Bulls, maybe instead, Steers, because their job is to steer us right, if you catch my cowhand lingo. Well, if he tried it, I think I'd blow the whistle on him to Father Rutuolo who'd give everybody the fisheye and tell them all that they're going to hell. But I have a lot of confidence that these cops are so into CPR that they'd probably tell him it's safer to watch porno on his TV with the binoculars. Forget I said that, Drinkie's no prude but she'd probably send him back up to the roof than to soil her living room with that stuff. There's no guarantee that if Fulmuna became a Hotalova, he'd eventually turn into a holy Hotski.

CHAPTER SIXTEEN

No Tello Rutuolo & Also That Vassily-o Fellow

Confidentially, that's what I like about the Catholic Priesthood. You can tell the Priest you hate yogurt and your secret will be safe with him, even if you like yogurt(!), which to me is a sin--don't worry, he won't blow your cover. I learned these last three words from American movies. But I don't think there's any penance to do, you know, prayers to say because of the sin of hating yogurt. But, the Roman Catholic church has changed alot, so who knows?

Ever wonder if the Priest keeps score? You know, how many confessions he heard that day? They could make those statistics mean something, because after all, the confessing people

(hey, I call them that because who am I to insult them by calling them sinners, which they all are, and more than me also, because they're the ones doing all the confessing, so they must be guilty. So, if I'm not, maybe I've got almost no sins, and then if I were Roman Catholic, why should I waste the time of the Priest with one or two? And what about carfare to the church? You know, it's like dirty laundry. I don't go to the Laundromat with one pair of dirty drawers--it makes no sense, does it? Let them collect, like maybe a month's worth, then I've got something to be concerned about. Otherwise I'll be wasting the Priest's time. Some people go to Confession every day, I think. Now, that's got to keep them on their knees and the Priest on his whatever he's leaning on to hear them.

He's got to lean on something, because it's got to be hard to take all that stuff standing up or even sitting down! Let's just say he's got to stay on his toes)

are really a picture of all of us! That's what we is, and that's what we are: sinners! Some more, some less, and of course then there is me, Stinko Ole, I'm different, right? Just think about my name. It's Rostinko Olevenkoskayad! Why couldn't people have called me "Rosti Ole"? No! They like "Stinko" better. And I guess if "Rostinko" was my last name, they'd have called me "Old Stinko" instead of "Ole Stinko"! But, I'm too young for that, now. Maybe we should all be called "Stinko", but then you couldn't tell who we're talking about, without giving us numbers, like "Stinko #7", "Stinko #9", etc. Just remember, I'm Stinko #1.

I can imagine without getting too graphic--that's another good word I learned--what the Priest's weekly scorecard might look like:

Greed	735
Lies	1,076
Theft	63
Hates	2,642
Cheating	1,115
Sloth	841
Gluttony	2,030
Idolatry	183
Envy	1,102
Vengeful & Spiteful acts, incl. Flatulence	93
Profanity, incl. middle fingers	48,633
Sex-related	173,648 & 1/2

Boy, after hearing all that stuff, he needs some kind of therapy, maybe a good massage, but not from Boring Boris Dimitrov!

Get an earful of this:

There we were, me and Drinkie, stoop-bound, as usual. And up comes Isabella with a half-gallon of Cherry-Vanilla ice cream which has to get up to her freezer. But she wants to hear about the war between Bulgaria and the Ukraine which almost began here the other day. I told her about the Bulgarian Bulge getting into trouble with some Ukrainian guys with his massage business, and how I think we saved his life because of lying, which I know was wrong, but I'm not as advanced in holy stuff like Tamara, and now Holy Hotski, the Evangelist, but I was glad to get those Ukrainian gorillas off the trail of the Bulge-o before they added to his bumps with black and blue souvenirs and maybe seven years bad luck after smashing every mirror in his "salon" upstairs, including the ceiling ones that I always worry about. This is what I wanted to tell you about in the last chapter about dodging a bullet. Here's what happened:

Bulging Bulgarian Boris Dimitrov meets this fat Ukrainian woman who couldn't bend down to pick up a load made by her skinny white Wolfhound. What a sight it was! Me and Fulmuna see her by the curb. The dog, who looks like an escapee from a Gulag--you know what that is, right?--dropped a huge load you'd expect from a Great Dane or Saint Bernard, and her pooper-scooper fell from her hand and a car coming in for a landing rolls right over the shaft, and goodbye pooper-scooper shaft. She is trying to bend down and get the fly-meal up with what's left of the scooper, and Bulge-o is coming toward the building, but then goes to her aid to do a good deed--let's not think something more. But somehow, after he helps her and pets her dog, of course, he picks up a new client, and with a lot to work on! How do I know? After a few minutes, she disappears with the skeleton-dog and he nods to us as he makes his way in past the stoop.

About twenty minutes later, the woman--let me not call her "fat Ukrainian", out of respect for those with so much more weight on them than most bones desire. Now look, it took me ten words to replace the word "fat"! How about two: exceedingly rotund. Check that in a dictionary, and if it doesn't appear in one of those pocket dictionaries, look for it in a fat one.

Let's try that again: about twenty minutes later, the exceedingly rotund woman--her name "Ivana", pronounced like "Ivana lose weight", comes past us on the stoop, made up nice, exotically perfumed, pretty face like Drinkie's only she's got matching sky-blue eyes, but the weight? What could I say? I didn't say it to Fulmuna who himself is exceedingly rotund--only a Russian-American can talk English the way most other Americans don't. Think I'm kidding? When is the last time you heard those two words except from me? Tell the truth, probably never! Maybe the NYPD would say it that way in a write-up so they don't get sued for verbal assault by using the unlawful word fat.

What didn't I say to Fulmuna? That Ivana could have passed for his sister, and if she had a sex-change, would fit very nicely into his clothes, and wouldn't have had a problem with the Bulge who I think prefers moving female flesh around than men's flesh.

Wait 'til you hear this: I counted three visits like in three strikes you're out at the old ball game, or three continuous strikes in bowling, which is called a Turkey. About an hour after the last visit, in which she left the building, crying and cursing in Russian, with things even I wouldn't say in Russian, and let me say, I can really curse bigtime in Russian, but then it's like war after that, unless I want to use those words on someone who doesn't know what I'm saying, especially when I say it in a nice tone. You know, like cursing at an animal in a pleasant tone. Now, where were we? Oh yes, an hour later from Ivana's exit, these three Ukrainian heavy-weight gorillas, though handsome and with crew cuts and beeg, beeg mossels-- that's right: not just muscles, but "mossels", as they pronounce them in English, came up to me and Fulmuna on the stoop and one says, "Excuse please, we luk for Boris, ees he home?" I figure he's toast if they get him, maybe even toasted bread crumbs, looking at how they were breathing, so I said "You just missed him, the police took him away, and they got his guns also! A very dangerous man. Who knew? He is wanted in Bulgaria for murdering husky women. They sealed off his apartment and said they're coming back to get more evidence. Can I help you? I'm Russky, I think you're Ukraine, right?"

And with that, they calmed down a bit and told us in Russian what happened, and afterwards I translated it for Fulmuna. The biggest mosselman was Ivana's brother Vassily, who said Boris had told his sister that having sex with him, Boris, that is, after a massage, would help her lose weight, and if she agreed, he would only charge her fifteen percent more. She then had asked him what he would charge if she were slim, and he told her if she were slim he wouldn't do it because he is a professional masseur, and only would do that with fat women because he feels sorry for them. Something about that ticked her off, or maybe the way he looked at her, who knows? But what got to me was big Vassily saying in English, catching on that Fulmuna didn't know Russian, "Eef my sistair want haf sax weet a peeg like that Bulgarian fok, I don't not care. Bot he want mek her pay! Dot is dorty treek! They weel take care of heem goot in Sofia!"

I don't like to write profanity in Russian or English, but the way he said the "F" word, I heard three letters not four, and if he tries to spell it in English, I think he'd use three because the "c" is silent. So that tells me I can get away with writing what he said. Nobody can accuse me of writing the four-letter word.

Anyhow, Vassily offered me a handshake and I shook hands with the other two "mosselmen". My last words with Vassily were an apology in Russian, telling him how sorry I was for Ivana's bad treatment, and that

I'd be glad to tell her so in person because we want to be good neighbors. I didn't say "neighbees" because there is no equivalent word for that in Russian or Ukrainian.

He then told me I was a very nice "mans" and glad I wasn't Bulgarian. Then he said Ivana is a nurse and lives in Wisconsin and would be flying back there in two more days. We said goodbye and they left. I think it was a good thing for the Bulge that we are his neighbees. Ful and I told him to stay out of sight for a week, and not to tell anybody in the neighborhood that he is a masseur or a Bulgarian. I also told him I had to lie to save his back parts--look how I can avoid cursing, even in Russian! I know Father Rutuolo would be proud of me; oh, and Tamara also! But because I had to lie to save the depraved Boris, I told the Drink and the Ful and Isabella, no tello Father Rutuolo or the beeg Ukrainian Vassily fellow. You see how good my English has gotten that I can even do good rhymes now! And you know, I don't think I had such a heavy accent like Vassily when I came here. Or, maybe I just forgot that I did?

That's what happens when you mix the wet and dry leaves and they get stuck together, not the Bulgarian way, either. Hey! I just thought of it. What happens if Vassily should ask the NYPD about Boris? I'll have my duck cooked! Oh, I think we say "goose", yes? Then I have to plan another lie, like it wasn't the cops but the FBI, and they didn't show the Bulge Courtesy, Professionalism, and Respect, because the slob didn't deserve it. I can tell them "slob" is okay as a four letter word, and much better than their three letter one which in Russian is ten letters. But look what happens! One lie leads to another! Ugh!

Be a good neighbee. No tello Father Rutuolo.

CHAPTER SEVENTEEN

El Pranko & Rutuolo The Fig-Dealer

So peaceful here on the stoop! How many times we just dozed off, me and Drinkie, Fulmuna, Isabella. Once Drinkie and me somehow conked out and were sleeping, our heads resting against each other's, with our mouths open, so we were told. Guess who woke us up? Nah, forget it! You'll never- -the NYPD! That's right. And you know who called them on us? You won't guess that one either. It was Boobie. I should give him a new title besides "Boob-head", maybe "El Pranko". I know he's more jealous of my friendship with Drinkie, than Fulmuna is! Yeah, Fulmuna, his peeping-partner, were off roof-duty because of a slight drizzle, besides, it was his day off, and I guess he wanted to make it memorable. He calls the cops, didn't hesitate, I'm sure, to tell them he thinks we have a suicide pact, and fears we've decided to check out on the stoop. Says he called us real loud, but was afraid to touch us because he didn't want his fingerprints found on either of us, and that he has a lot of superstition and other concerns about touching the dead, and said we looked real dead. I guess now I know we don't look like we're breathing when we sleep on the porch!

We were dry, of course, under the porch marquee, and that's what the El Pranko does for entertainment. And, the cops not only woke us up, but also shook us up! But then they called him to say we're okay, and he must have sounded like he's crying on the phone the way the cop seemed to be comforting him. He said he couldn't come down because he wasn't dressed, and I hear the officer say, "You're welcome, you're welcome; yes, I'm sure you'll see them tomorrow, if they're around." Well, that was

C_____ P_____ R_____

at its usual best. Nice guys, and a woman, too. She acted very nice but I got the feeling nobody should mess with her, you got my dog-whistle warning? Good. And good-looking Patrolwoman--I guess that's what we call them; I could have asked. Guess she's hoping to become an NYPD shrink because she asked us if we were on medication for depression, or taking any psycho-stimulants. Then, she asked if the suicide pact is a written document. What a bird that Boobie is! But I'm pretty quick on my mental feet, so I told her our "concerned neighbee" has a hearing problem and is also a busybody, and overheard us talking about the leaves by the sewer-side packed down because of rain, but all he heard was "sewer-side packed". Another lie! How I hate myself! No tello Rutuolo! Really wanted to tell the truth, like with the Bulgarian "Fok" who dissed the exceedingly rotund Sofia, and who knows what was on the Ukrainian menu if they got their catch of the day! So blowing the whistle of truth on the Boob-head would have really hurt Isabella, because he's the husband, and who knows who she thinks is the man, if not me! But after that, it definitely wouldn't be him!

There's gotta be a law against pranking, especially if it costs the victim or institution. There isn't one against neighbeeing because wet and dry leaves clumping together saves people from going down the drain, and that's why my mind is always in the gutter and the sewer. That doesn't sound right but you know what I mean, right? Say "Yes", but not too loud. You're supposed to be reading a book, not talking to it.

Well, on this peaceful, mild evening, guess who pops up, catching me, the Drink, and the Slutta-but-not-from-the-gutter-Isabella? There you go-- wrong again! Father Rutuolo! And, with a big bag of fresh figs somebody gave as a bribe to get into the local Roman Catholic section of Heaven, although the good Father is on to those moves--I should know, I played a lot of Scrabble with him. But if those figs are as good as they look, who knows what one can do for fig-specialists who know how to wrap their fig-tree in carpets to survive the winter? Grandpa Bert knows how to do all that stuff, but he's into basement bathtub mushrooms, not figs--go figure!

"Hello, stoop-sinners and heathens!" he says--what a sense of humor! "I figured I'd catch somebody on the stoop, but was hoping it would be Tamara. Anybody want some fresh figs? Help yourself! Go ahead, don't be shy!" he says, opening the shopping bag which smelled more of wine-making grapes than figs. So, we all begged off; then Isabella asks him if he's going to make "fig-newtons", a kind of cookie filled with crushed figs in a paste. And he tells her to stay away from those things because they're too sweet and rotted a few of his teeth years ago. He said if he were Pope, eating them would be declared a mortal sin--what a funny Priest! Of course I put in my two cents and said if the Pope did that, knowing human nature, the sale of fig-newtons would go through the roof! And, what does he come back with? "Rostinko, my son, I've been saying for years now, too bad you're a heathen, you'd make a good Priest!" Always trying to catch me, always! The guy is good, then he got me back to the main course: "Is Tamara okay? Haven't seen her in several weeks. Sent her a letter, called and left messages on her machine. Have you seen her?" Obviously, he didn't read this book yet, because Chapter 14 would have given him some ideas on her. Then, he adds, "How ironic that I get postcards regularly from the Mendels, you remember Morris with Sydelle, the chain-smoker, alias our Scrabble-partner with the smoking machine? But I get nothing from Tamara, not even a return phone call!"

So, Drinkie gives me the elbow while Isabella is going gently through the fig-bag, having changed her figgle-mind--like that, hah?--from one fig to the next. "Speak, Stink--you're the man!" she says. The good Father looks up from the bag: "You know something, Rostinko?" "I do, Father, but please don't say I told you." I answered. "Worry not, my son, I'll consider it a confession!" That was as good as a certified check to me, so I told him about the Hotski, and that she'd been dating him some weeks now, since they're not living together, and has been going to his church with him and probably didn't want to say anything. I expected a frown or some other bad reaction, but he went into another dimension. He puts down the fig-bag, raises his hands and says, "Bless You, Father! Bless You!" I thought the Roman Catholics were big on the Virgin Mary and their saints, but he was cutting out the middle-men, and went right to the Source. Then, his voice cracked, his hands were shaking and he barely got out, "Oh, God! What a miracle, what a miracle! Thank you, thank you, Father!" Then he whips out this big blue-striped bandana, wipes his eyes, slaps a meathook on my shoulders and says "My son, you've made me richer tonight with that news than a cargotainer of figs!"

I notice Isabella still standing with figs in both hands, sort of struck dumb, and Drinkie is covering her face. I got the feeling he had much more invested in the Yestadeys than we did. Then Isabella said, "Gee, Reverend, I thought you'd be upset about maybe losing one of your parishioners." And he, still working over his cheeks with the bandana, shakes his head, "No, no, my child, this sounds to me like a sheep come home, I only hope he's not caught up in a cult. I'm going to think the best!"

Then, Drinkie looks up with her two beautiful different-colored eyes, and says, "Stinko is the man, but you're really the Priest, Father, really!" And he smiles at us and nods his head up and down, then side to side as if saying "Yes" and "No", but I got the feeling he was sneaking in a sign of the Cross without telling the heathens before him--and then picks up the fig-bag with one hand, and with the other, thumb and index finger touching, smiles largely and says, "Ecumenism! Ecumenism!", looks up at the starry night sky, then says, "Good night, children, you've made my day!" Then I stopped him with "Oh, uh, Father Rutuolo, do you think they'll get together again?" And he comes back with "First the trust, then the trousseau! Let Him do it, not us and they'll be clumping together again like wet and dry leaves in the gutter! Isn't that your eccentric but interesting parable, Rostinko?" And away he went into the night, not waiting an answer to that one. What could I say except that these Priests and Pastors are sort of like spiritual NYPD guys making Courtesy, Professionalism, and Respect to be instead, Charity, Prayer, and Reverence their motto.

You know, I caught that big word "Ecumenism", but had trouble even figuring out what "trousseau" was, even in Russian, but then the Drink gave me an education and made me feel good saying it's the kind of word women know about, but men probably think it's a French dessert. So, I left it there. I don't have to know everything.

Anyway, you get it, I think, it's good stuff, not French dessert although that too, but I'm talking about Ecumenism, and how we need it, get my drift? You know, respect one another's faith-ideas, even if we believe something else? That is, as long as Society is not hurt by somebody's beliefs. Anyway, I think the Jesus crowd has the edge on them all, but I won't tell that to Hotski, he's liable to have his Holy-Roller squad, including the ones in front of the Deli across the street, go to work on me. I don't know, maybe that's what I need. Oops, slipped again! Almost repeated myself How about "connect my asterisks" instead of my "drift" tag. I would have said "dots" but don't want to repeat myself with that one, either. Anyway, I think it might be good to bring the dictionary down when I do my stoop duty, so I can look up things like "trousseau" right away and compare it with Drinkie's vague definition. She won't mind, and besides, sitting on the book could avoid my sticking to the stoop and maybe I'll be absorbing some more knowledge where Boobie told me not too long ago he thinks my brains are. What a fink! Now, I've got to check that one in the dictionary! But no matter, that's him anyway!

CHAPTER EIGHTEEN

El Hammo & The Backfiring Boffo

You know, I didn't tell you much about every other tenant here. First, because I think some of them are ghosts--whoever sees them? But there's one guy who thinks he's "The Continental". Picture this guy: about six one, kinda slim, looks like an old Peter O'Toole, the actor, and is very dramatic. Why? Because he's an actor with no job. He says "Between assignments". Wow! To me, sounds like the title of a 1930's British movie. Why can't he just say "Unemployed"--is that so bad? Perhaps, how about "I'm between having no job and looking for a job, which means I've got no job but I can't have one until I get one, which I hope will happen soon!" Now, that's got to be about thirty words at least. If he says it often enough, he'll never get a job because he's using all his time talking about it without talking about it, instead of looking for it! Get my drift? Good.

Now, here's a little more on "El Hammo" or "il Hammo" depending in which country you place him: He's very dramatic like as if he's on stage. Just about everything he says is a quote from some classical play or book, and it just comes out of him like he's in the middle of a performance, if you get the scene. I think we once had a President like that, but can't remember where I read about it--so full of himself, or some other substance, and maybe there's no difference between them.

Anyway, three weeks ago, Hammo is sitting on the stoop next to "Boffo", a big teddy bear of a dog, I think part Chow and part something else, maybe a Saint Bernard. Now, Boffo loves beans, so his owner who lives next door to Durham Perigord--that's the Actor's name, I just remembered it--buys a lot of beans in the Ninety-nine cent stores, because it's cheaper than dog food, he says, and better for him. I think you know what's coming, right? So, Boffo is down by us with his master, Hennie McManus. I'm on the stoop sitting on the top step next to McManus, and Boffo is waiting to be curbed--you know, like to make.

Durham, the "Ham"--that's what I call him between a few "Hammo" 's here and there when his name comes up--wait, hold on a sec. I know a little geography so, I get "Perigord" as a last name. It's a French Province famous for food and wine and guess what? Yeah, Truffles! Now that you know all about them, right? Remember, Alba Madonnas? Grandpa Bert's basement bathtubs? That's right, just a few chapters back. So know this: they don't trifle with Truffles in Perigord. Anyway, I guess Hammo's father or grandfather came from there. What about "Durham"? Probably that's from the Mother who must've had roots in Durham, North Carolina or the city Durham in North East England which is in County Durham there. I'm betting it is the English connection because he sounds like Shakespeare's first cousin who we all thought would be dead by now. Who can figure the French connection? Don't ask him in front of the building when I'm around--I ain't gonna ask him either, because he's liable to start quoting lines from Les Miserables in French and will draw an audience in front of Bergie's building here. It's not the place for auditions or theatre.

Speaking of what's in a name, Grandpa Bert calls him "The Continental". Now really, nobody today knows about "The Continental" except for Umberto Dellacroce, Drinkie's Grandpa, because that was back about 1950 and "The Continental" was Renzo Cesana, with a TV show that was just him talking to the viewer like Mr. Rogers did with the kids on TV, changing clothes and all in front of the camera, but I think the show was in the evening like about eleven, and he, Renzo, The Continental, talked to women watching the show in their bedrooms and he got them all thrilled in fantasyland while their slug or mug of a husband snored like a hibernating bear with the ripped pajamas and all the other slobby things that put them at a great disadvantage compared with "Mr. Hormones" oozing out of the picture tube unto their kissable bare feet, heating up their bunions and putting them in the mood for a midnight Tango--if you catch my sizzle--sounds better than "drift", yes? And Umberto, who has an Italian accent after over seventy-five years here, said Renzo had a real Italian accent, so I guess it was as thick as Contadina tomato paste.

Now, where were we? Oh yes, Durham is throwing out one of his pet quotes, and as usual tells us where it comes from first, and I've just about got it memorized having heard it kind of like all the time, it seems, if you follow my enthusiasm:

" 'Imitation of Horace, Book Three, Ode 29; speaking of fortune: I can enjoy her while she's kind, but when she dances in the wind, and shakes the wings and will not stay, I puff the prostitute away.' "

And just then, like on cue, Boffo who was sitting next to El Hammo, stands on all fours, making his bomb bay level with the actor's left ear-- all accidental of course--lifts his big whip of a tail, and rolls out a classic invisible bomb--talk about a "boffo"! And Durham's ear gets the full force of the blast, his nose--the gas, and he jumps to his feet as if a big dog just flatumigated in his ear--which he did--and throws his left hand over his ear, yelling, "Oh, my God! This bitch almost broke my eardrum--it's still ringing!"

McManus, not wasting a second, runs Boffo to the curb for a dump, if you know what that is, like for a hint it comes out of the back end of a dog, and all the time shouting back, "I'm sorry, so sorry Durham, he had to go. I shouldn't have lingered--so sorry!" And then, "El Hammo", like in a miraculous reversal of roles from victim to victor, throws out,

"Thomas Love Peacock--The Misfortunes of Elphin, translated from the Welsh, chapter three: 'Not drunk is he who from the floor, can rise alone and still drink more; but drunk is he who prostrate lies, without the power to drink or rise.' " With that, he walks past McManus, pats him on the can, says "Ta ta, Hennie, and lay the assault to Boffo's charge, not yours, dear neighbee--brute beast that he is!"

How I remember these things just about word for word amazes me, especially because I looked up the Peacock quote to verify it. I think it's because of the way Durham throws out these lines with all his body language—something to see! I guess if you want to remember a phone number, ask El Hammo to say it a few times and you'll probably never forget it, including him, maybe even El Boffo. Hey, that's how it is with good neighbees, them and their stuff is so memorable, like clumps of wet and dry leaves stuck together on the drainholes of the sewer grate at the end of the curb gutter in the street.

Of course, McManus, being the conscientious neighbee and good citizen, makes sort of a glove out of the Pathmark plastic bag he had in his pocket, and picks up Boffo's bean factory produce, warm, moist, and pungent as the breath of an aging actor between assignments--if you catch my--no, Boffo's whiff. There's no diff, and they call me "Stinko"!

And just for the record, Boffo is no "bitch", and perhaps because of the size of his "exit produce"(e.p.), a name closely resembling "bitch" would be fittingly descriptive.

(now, who else you ever read could say the four-lettered "s" word with such class? Doesn't that beat "b.m." by a mile? Of course, it is not without unintended consequences. Were one to teach a child to say e.p. instead of b.m., others within earshot might think the child suffering from apraxia or dyspraxia or be in the budding stages of dyslexia and referring to the water of man not the duty of man. Once again, don't you marvel at the sophistication of the narrator for not succumbing to vulgar descriptions of body excretions? Not that I'm not humble, which I'm not, but the name "Stinko" is far more elite than one would think! Not only that, but don't you sort of wonder if this book is being ghost-written when you hear this smart stuff coming out. This is real e.p., is it not?)

So, back to Boffo's back end e.p.. Being a "He", "bitch" is inaccurate. Perhaps "batch" or "batcher" works with logic, and sort of gets in the lack of pedigree idea without having to call him a "batchard" with his e.p. stuff and its dimensions. This is complex reasoning, and I'm trying to be as classy as I can without resorting to the easy use of vulgarities. Getting better at it, did you notice?

And, did you also notice that not once did you hear El Hammo mention calling 911 because of the rear assault--or maybe the "rear ear" assault by El Boffo? In a way, I just wonder, could the whammo on El Hammo be a payback for him gassing off in all our ears? Maybe, maybe. But so what? With all these money-monsters around today, they could make a lawsuit about a fortune cookie and strike it rich. No, that's not the way a true neighbee does it. Gotta hand it to El Hammo. I think after the show he's the real deal and has the mark of a true neighbee, who doesn't need to waste the time of the NYPD who probably would have come anyway to give emergency CPR to El Hammo along with some "Beano" infusion and a few dog treats, and you know what CPR means, so be careful not to confuse the NYPD with the EMS's idea of CPR. Get it? Got it? Good.

And, by the way, curbing El Boffo, is one thing, but McManus also bags it after it hits the gutter, whether or not anybody is looking, because otherwise, a soaking rainfall could float it past us down the drainholes where we leaves are clumping together--another good law-abiding neighbee!

CHAPTER NINETEEN

In The Pincus

If it were up to Marcus and Mitzi Pincus, the world would be free of all disease. They had a drug in their health food store for every sickness, every condition, every situation known to man and beast. Either come to Happy Health Haven at 73-20 Mavan Boulevard and be assured of a cure even if you have to keep buying their stuff 'til you die of what is supposed to be fixed, or come to Apt. 3E and they'll sell it to you in the foyer.

After listening to Marcus the Barker and Mitzi the Echo, I got the feeling they had pills for broken legs, creams for stolen wallets, and syrups for fender benders. You think I'm kidding, right? Just listen to them five minutes and the world could be healed of everything by what's in their store or that they might have to order. I think they have a pill for death, but are not allowed to sell it over the counter because it cuts into the Funeral business. And the fine people running those places do not like making trouble--if you catch my high fly ball to center field.

Before they moved into our building complex, I was in their shop looking for a paperback on bean recipes. Mitzi the echo has put on her other hat, Mitzi The Brain Surgeon, and is curing some gentle soul's excruciating migraines with a sale on a five pound protein powder food supplement. I got the feeling he came down with the migraine after asking a question about something else. Then, as I'm spinning the revolving rack to find the bean book, I'm hearing Marcus the Witch doctor pitch something called Vitamin B15, Pangamic acid and another winner called Co-Enzyme Q10, to a woman who told them she is 99. She looks 97, but what do I know? She asked for some vitaminized lipstick, for her dry lips, but at that age you'd think it better to just keep licking your lips or just eat the stuff. Now, I've got nothing against being that old and trying to help yourself, but wouldn't you think by 90 at least you'd suspect that Marcus was too young to tell you how to become 100?

Maybe, instead he could have asked her what she was taking and then order some of that stuff, take it yourself and push it on all those sick-looking people who live in health food stores.

Anyway, Dr. Hocus Pincus, oops, sorry, Marcus Pincus, whips out the B15 and the Q10--sounds like the Brooklyn and Queens bus lines--and says, "I refuse to carry that lipstick anymore because it's under investigation for false claims!" The vitaminarian's jaw dropped, and I could see she had pretty good choppers, the bottom row anyway, and just exhaled at him with "Huh!"

Pincus then went into his full customer support mode: "Take them, Mrs. Hull, they'll get you to 105! Believe me, I know!" And she answered, "But what about my dry lips? I don't want to use that toxic lip wax they advertise." she pleaded. Now the Marcus really went into overdrive: "Mrs. Hull, may I call you Beatrice?", a big warm smile breaking out over his confident, nutritional-expert face. She returned the smile, her 99 year-old lips not cracking, and he continued the pitch: "It is the combination of what you ingest that gives you the benefit." Sometimes I have a hard time deciding what to call the things some people say, but when they sling it with style like Marcus and Mitzi, the Great Nutrition dance team, the words, the images become branded in my nutrient-deficient brain.

Suddenly he whips out a carob bar and says, "Bea, I'm going to share a secret with you--don't say I told you--sometimes these things I say get back to manufacturers--I don't want any trouble, do you?" She inclines backward a bit because he's doing a number on her with the beady black eyeballs over the steel-rimmed bifocals, the wiggling, bushy reddish-greyed eyebrows making their Groucho Marx hootchee cootchees at her, and in a soft voice, she peeps, "No!"

And here's the killer deal-closer: "Beatrice, you're a walking success! I want an invitation to your 100th Birthday party if you have one, and this is going to help you make it! Take one B15 and one Q10 once daily with food. After a half-hour, break off one slotted piece of the carob bar, let it melt in your mouth, then lick your lips with the carob-bean tongue--yours, not some Caribbean's--and don't clean it off for three hours. If anybody sees you, tell them you're wearing carob-bean lipstick--you'll be telling them the truth." "Ohhh, Dr. Marcus, I like that! I wish I knew this when I was younger!" she says, beaming about such a revelation. And of course, the Marcus is full of non-profit encouragement: "Never too late to start, my dear!" "Ching!" I could hear the old cash register with the bell sounding off as the dollar signs rolled in the eyes of Marcus & Mitzi like a slot machine in Atlantic City, if you catch what I'm drawing here.

This made me hungry for one of those bars, and zap! Just like that, Lady Beatrice is reaching to open her bag, "And how much do I owe you, Dr. Marcus? Now he goes into stage 2. Bending slightly as if the Queen of England is before him, he closes his eyes, one hand on his mid-section: "Beatrice, Beatrice......". Boy, was he into the part! It could have been "Romeo, Romeo", the way the dramatics were dripping. He was almost as good as El Hammo! "A woman such as you is to be honored. The carob bar is my gift." "Oh no, I--", she began to protest. He cut her off with "and for you, the B15 and Q10 are half-price--that's almost my cost, but I'm investing in you as a living example of a successful longevity, and we're only half-way there!" "Half-way there?" I thought to myself, this guy not only slings it, but is now trying to install her in the Guinness book of records for long-living! This was no ordinary horse manure. We're talking thoroughbred!

With that she pulls out a fifty from her purse, saying "Here, keep the change, unless it's not enough?" The modest Marcus reassures her, "No, no dear Bea, you're too generous. Thirty-five is plenty. Let me give you change." She abruptly says, "No! I insist. How about instead giving it to me in carob bars? That will save me steps. I think I'll be liking this lip-coating therapy very much!" Again with the eyebrows and royal bowing. The stuff goes into a Happy Health Haven transparent shopping bag with photo of the good Doctor and Mitzi on it.

The Mitzi comes to the counter and leaves her with "You look so good, Mrs. Hull, whatever you're taking, please don't stop." And Marcus chimes in: "And now she's going to take Pangamic acid and Co-Enzyme Q10 also!" Mitzi then nods positively and does "Oh, Doctor, the Pangamic! That's wonnnnderful!" More nodding, some "Mmmm"'s, then Mitzi spots all the carob bars in the bag, seems to levitate (didn't think I knew that word, being a Slav, hah?), reaches with both hands as if to either adjust her bra or pinch her own armpits, then flaps her elbows like she's doing the Chicken dance, "The acid with the Q10 and the carob! Mrs. Hull, you're something else!" Beatrice is beginning to look a little unsteady, maybe from all this excitement at the Happy Health Haven, "But Dr. Mitzi, this is the recommendation of Dr. Marcus!" Now, I'm starting to wonder why I can't be called "Dr. Stinko", that's also four syllables.

So now it was time for me to put in my two cents, being too distracted by all this nutritional therapy to find the bean book. This was a live Pincus team performance. How often could I hope to see something like that? Besides, I was now convinced I needed what Mrs. Hull was prescribed, in order to survive to 105, but not as fast as she was going to get there. Approaching the three-person convention at the counter, I said, "Excuse me, people, I also want to do the B15 with the Q10 and the carob treatment, I like that number 99!" "Well, look at that!" Mrs. Hull remarked, while Marcus nodded with a pleasant cash register look. With that, Mitzi gives Beatrice a peck on the cheek, proving she really is a chicken, and pats her arm affectionately, as the dear, almost-100 lady leaves the store with a smile. This is returned with a Pincus duet of "Be well, Mrs. Hull. See how much good we can do without even knowing it somehow?"

Well, here I am, far from 105. Probably too far, but in no hurry to get there anyway. A while back I ran out of B15 and Q10 and have maybe one piece of carob buried under something, and now that the Pincus's have lived here a while, I wonder if there is a memory drug that really works, because aside from knowing me as a neighbee, they never mention seeing me in the store that day with Mrs. Hull, and I never went back. Nothing wrong, just the way life is. Anyhow, with their magical marketing duo skill, all is well with the world.

Magic or not, I don't think they have a pill for Courtesy, Love, and Respect, and neither does the NYPD who does Professionalism instead of Love--they have to, of course, and I'm sure the Pincus magic will cough up a free carob bar now and then, to show them we appreciate them. I know the other neighbors do, and they saw how fast the NYPD was on the job when Count Maritza was teaching violin on the couch. Poor Vilia, I still remember that little pink-eyed rat. Somehow it goes with the name "Pincus". Even wings wouldn't have saved her. But she was hit by the Cross so I think she got them, if you catch my religious smarts about animal afterlife. But anyway, may the Force be with us human rats 'til 105. I'm talking about the NYPD (just kidding, boys and girls in the blue, just kidding, unless you're not hoping to retire one day). And let's not twist words, we're the rats, the CPR team are the cats. Stay in line and you can eat all the cheese you want, but do something fishy and bingo! they'll be on your trail like Pac man, remember him?

And I know we want to keep our streets clean with all that alternate side of the street parking, but I think if we all clumped together like wet and dry leaves, stuck on the drainholes of the steel sewer grate at the end of the curb gutter in the street, then the neighborhood wouldn't go down the drain either, and the Sanitation guys could do other sanitizing than with the trucks swirling those big circular brushes which really hurt when you're clumping on the sewer grate.

CHAPTER TWENTY

Room For Neighbees, Mushrooms, And Foster Children

On The Way To One Hundred And Thirty

So, here I am, by the gutter but not in it. It rained last night, and I'm waiting for Isabella to come down, you know, Isabella Slutta, Boobie's wife? He apologized to me again last night for his latest flare-up which I told you about, I think, but who knows? Isabella asked me to go with her to the doctor, because she thinks she's going through her changes. She's about fifty-four, I think, and Boobie's sleeping and is trusting me again, but who knows for how long, and now she tells me a strange thing: she got him to agree to seeing if they can take in a foster child. I didn't ask why, but when she asked what I thought, I just popped off with "Wow! A baby neighbee!"

And she said, "You know, Stinko, I think we got something good going here, and it's got to end sometime; so if this is good for us, it's gonna be good for that kid--if we get approved; and Drinkie's Grandpa Bert is getting kinda close to three digits, I don't have to tell you. I know you think he's good for one hundred and thirty, but have you ever heard of anybody living that long? And also, how old will we be twenty-seven years from now? What if we croak? So, I like the idea of sharing some of our good life with some kid who could use it, before we all push up the mushrooms, yes? And speaking of mushrooms, did you ever wonder if maybe Grandpa Bert is going to make it to one hundred and thirty because of those mushrooms?"

Now, I don't have a clue why she picked "twenty-seven", but some simple addition would have given her the answer. Maybe she's thinking about frogs since she thinks we could croak? How long do they live? One thing I know, they usually die before their next birthday unless they die on it. That's one of ole Grandpa Bert's pearls of wisdom. For some reason, it bothers me every time I try to figure it out. I'm afraid if I ask him how he comes to that knowledge, he's liable to tell me something else I can't figure out. I'd rather appear smart to him and just nod my head. You're probably doing the same right now, yes?

She really got me thinking that the Alba Madonnas could be his fountain of youth, you know, like the Spanish guy in Florida, Ponce de Leon? Who knows if that was true about the water he was looking for? Suppose it was mushrooms and he kept it to himself so he could sell them without competition? I can picture him there in the Everglades, letting his men risk an alligator pedicure checking out the waters there, while he keeps sneaking off into the brush, telling them he's going to take care of business--you notice what class I've got, getting better every day! I could have easily said, he went to take a--oops! See why I don't like to explain too much?

Anyway, you get the idea, it was mushrooms! Alba Madonnas, possibly! The secret of eternal life, or at least reaching Grandpa Dellacroce's ninety-three--we'll have to keep an eye on him, and if he makes it to one hundred and thirty, it's the mushrooms. What else could it be? Don't forget also the Bergs! Maggie with the flaming eyes, and they live on those mushrooms! Who knows, the stuff may also be breast enhancers, "Pontoons de Leons!" There you go! That's it! Forget about implants, do the mushroom plant! And for sure, when Grandpa Bert pushes up the mushrooms, it will be because Drinkie agreed to let him stay home for his own funeral, in the bathtub! Makes all the sense in the world and in the cellar! Wow! Look at that! We found the secret of longevity just by letting the words flow to the paper, and I haven't even eaten one of those mushrooms yet!

Well, it sure is time to start while I'm this young before I get any older. And maybe we can get everybody in the building to eat them so we can be neighbees for as long as we live, and maybe that will mean a hundred and thirty or maybe more. Hey, I read about those Bible guys, like Abraham and his ancestors. Maybe it was mushrooms? I'll have to check that out again with Hotalova's big Bible. I wonder if he knows anything about what

I'm saying here? Maybe I'll let him see this book when it gets printed. I think he can handle it. Why not? All I did was give folks the scoop about us neighbees! If they should drop in sometime I'll get Grandpa Bert to show them his mushroom factory! They gotta be Kosher, right? Bergie wouldn't eat them otherwise. For sure, poison mushrooms are not approved for Passover, but maybe in certain situations they are. Never can be too sure. Always pays to check first. I know it sounds crazy, but Grandpa Bert once told me Locusts are Kosher! He says it's in the Bible. Locusts Kosher? It blew me away! Yeah, I can picture him in Kalish's Meat Market looking in the cold shelves section where they have the insect meats, yeah, right away, or maybe him and Magdalena, to bury some in the bathtubs; gotta be good for the ground, with all the crops they eat, right? But what if one of those locusts keeled over because it ate a poison mushroom, and then we eat it? That's Kosher, right? If my gears are meshing, I think the Rabbi has to teach me about that one.

And with all these thoughts rapid-firing in my brain like the gunfight at the OK Corral, there I was, the only one left standing, with Isabella looking at me, like I was somewhere else, like in the Florida Everglades four hundred years ago. With that I just hugged her right there by the gutter and said, "Isabella, you and Drinkie and Tamara are the women, and Boobie and Fulmuna and Hotalova are the husbands, and I'm the man, and here we be like clumps of wet and dry leaves stuck together on the drainholes of the sewer grate at the end of the curb gutter in the street!" Just then, from Isabella's living room window, is Boobie, with what looks like no clothes on, shaking a fist and yelling, "Wait for me, Stinkface! I'm coming right down, I saw you!" "Boobie," I shouted, ready to make peace by yelling "it's the mushrooms!" even though that wouldn't have meant anything to him. Anyway, Isabella cut in, yelling up to him, "You better put some clothes on, Jerko, because we're both gonna give it to you!" With that she says, "Let's go, Stink, before we have to keep my word--he never learns!" So, I said, "Well, look Isabella, you are something special to gaze at." With that she squeezes my arm and smiles saying "Stinko, I love you more than a brother like neighbees should, with--how does that go? Love, Courtesy, and Respect, not like the NYPD who do Professionalism instead of love, which is okay because we need that too, like for the jerk up in the window, getting a suntan while he foams at the mouth with everything hanging out!" So, I moved real quick and she says, classic Isabella, that is, "Ah, don't sweat it, Stink--he's just a big boobie!"

Now, even though I'm "dissipated", as Drinkie's Aunt Philomena says about me because I haven't worked in a while, Isabella's got me thinking maybe I could do some volunteer work with kids, you know, adopt a whole bunch of them on a regular part time basis? Then it hit me: "Oh! Isabella, I should have told Drinkie what's happening, she's gonna be looking for me!" And Isabella slapped me back to my senses with her tongue, "Don't sweat it, Stinko, she's an understanding wife--good thing for Fulmuna, and better than that, she's a neighbee! Call her on the cellphone if you think you have to!"

So there, by now you can see how we live together, love together, and help together, even when life changes, just like good neighbees should, like clumps of--by now you should be able to complete the sentence, if you get my drift, that is, my metaphorical impression. It just doesn't get any better, no better, no way Jose-ay, as I think they say down Mexico way. Up here they say: "Ole!" And that's me.

Stinko

Conclusion

Soooooo, there you have it. That's what is across the street. Heard Stinko real clear, didn't you? And did you notice how much he improved about repeating himself. Not an easy feat considering the bunch of unusual creatures he lives with--that's Neighbees for you.

I think we agree they're all eccentric bees, and Stinko's wiring isn't according to code either. I mean, he's so fixated on leaves "clumping" on the sewer grate--what's that all about? Maybe I should read his first chapter again, or maybe the rest of them.

Oh, and then there's his fixation with the NYPD. Something's cooking there, possibly some crime he thought he got away with way back when, and it's haunting his conscience? Ahah! Maybe I can apply for a job as a Cold Case Investigator. I'll think about it.

Anyway, I can't believe, can't accept what is gnawing away in my subconscious, and just can't let you go without dropping this notion on you: that maybe all this screwy Neighbee stuff is about us, all of us, and maybe we need to broaden our "elite" definition of what "normal" is. Who do we call to do that? Let's start with the NYPD. At least I'm sure we'll get CPR from them, is that C L e a R? Maybe? Yep, I think so.

Jim